Dedication

To my Mother and Father for their love and wisdom.
To my Wife for her love and understanding.
To my Friends for their love and support.
God Bless You All.

Douglas E. Glaeser

Author's Note

Nowhere was the undertaking of writing this book to be found on my radar when I look back on the many goals I had set for myself. Over the years, whenever I would relate my stories to friends, the reaction would always be the same; "*You should write a book.*" After more than a decade of hearing this again and again, I finally picked up a pen and started to write. I'm glad I did.

Writing this book was a tremendous, personal experience; almost cathartic. This is an opportunity to help people be more successful in their careers and lives by sharing my experiences. I've never been one for wasting people's time; as you will soon discover. This book is by no means a text book...it's a survival guide...filled with humorous and insightful *slices of life, how to(s), and do not(s)*.

There is no getting away from the simple fact that work is a necessity if we aspire to acquire even a few creature comforts along the way. Whether you're a veteran of the workplace or a novice, there's no escaping that each of us will have to deal with an *idiot* or two on the job. This book will teach you how to cope, survive, and advance.

Today, it is becoming more and more difficult to find "the simple joys of life" due to the hectic schedules and demands that even the most simplistic life can impose. Home, work, and children can take a considerable amount of energy. Throw in a monkey wrench or two into the mix, and it can lead to utter chaos; making it all the more important that you don't allow *idiots* to place additional stress, if it can be avoided. And, it can be, but it takes being forearmed.

I've been very fortunate during my lifetime to have had the benefit of mentors; foremost were my parents, a small number of exceptional school teachers and college professors, and a few extraordinary business people. And, so when it became my turn to take the reins, I mentored whenever an opportunity presented itself on the job. Writing this book is a way to reach more people than I could ever hope to reach through my consulting practice.

I want this book to be more than simply pointing out troublesome personalities in the workplace. I want it to provide the "nuts 'n bolts" to important workplace topics. Lessons one could learn and implement to advance one's career. So, in that regard, I've included chapters on leadership, negotiation, salesmanship, business etiquette, communications, interviewing and many other day-to-day essential skills; chapters not necessarily idiot related, but important nonetheless.

This book is really *two* books in *one*. In many chapters, I interlace stories between my business and personal life experiences. I did this because...*who you are...is who you are*. Very seldom is there a distinction between how one conducts themselves at home and at work. My personal life stories will help you to have a better understanding of how I became who I am and why I conduct myself as I do.

Throughout this book, I also interchange the word *you* and the word *one*. Examples: *You* should never...or...*One* should never ...I purposely made this distinction when referencing *you* when I felt it was appropriate to do so...as opposed to my addressing the general populace with the word *one* when correcting behavior. After all, I don't know you. Not everyone is an *idiot*.

The web site shown below is not only where one can direct family and friends to purchase their own copy of the book, it's where readers can post and exchange their encounters with idiots. I am sure that many of you have your share of funny and interesting stories from *your* work experiences. It would be great to hear from you.

How many idiots does it take to change a light bulb? The answer is in the pages that await you. Enjoy.

www.WorkingWithIdiots.net

Table of Contents

Chapter One – *Don't Worry, Be Happy*
Idiots are all around us; above, below and across the aisle. Learn to recognize them.

Chapter Two – *It Was a Very Good Year*
What makes the author of this book tick? Here's a little history courtesy of "yours truly".

Chapter Three – *Back Stabbers*
People wear many disguises. See how many personality types you can identify.

Chapter Four – *Who Will Buy*
We're all selling something; from your skills on a resume to an old, beat-up dresser at a yard sale. Here are some techniques that can help.

Chapter Five – *Getting To Know You*
Landing that big promotion or a new job can be a challenge; the better prepared, the better the chances for success.

Chapter Six – *Just the Way You Are*
Perception is the great equalizer; but perceptions can mislead. Make sure you are seeing things clearly.

Chapter Seven – *You've Got to Be Taught*
Much of today's political correctness is just plain political craziness. Learn how to maintain your sanity.

Chapter Eight – *The Meeting Song*
One too many meetings on your calendar? Meetings to plan meetings? There is a better way to manage this onslaught.

A Lifetime

Working with Idiots
&
How to Survive

- Insights from a Self-Made Man -

Douglas E. Glaeser

Chapter One – "Don't Worry, Be Happy"

In every life, we have some trouble. When you worry, you make it double.

Call me Ishmael.

The sentence above is one of the most recognizable first lines in all of literature. My college English Professor would be proud of me. While that sentence has absolutely no bearing on the content of this book, it does meet the "number one" requirement for Creative Writing 101; the first sentence must command the reader's attention. Now that I have yours, let's begin.

The Merriam-Webster Dictionary defines an idiot as: a stupid person; a fool - imbecile - blockhead - dunce - nitwit - dolt - moron - jerk - dimwit - airhead - simpleton - and on and on. I believe the word idiot has more synonyms than any other word in the English language. My favorite idiot quote goes: "Suppose you were an idiot, and suppose you were a member of Congress; but I repeat myself." - Mark Twain.

For those of you old enough to remember the opening mono-logue for the television series **Dragnet**, "the stories you are about to hear are true. The names have been changed to protect the innocent." The stories in this book are analogous. This book was written on the premise that you, the reader, are not an idiot. However, if, during the course of your reading, you discover that you possess traits of idiocy, save yourself and, even more importantly, save those around you from *you*. This will be a perfect opportunity to redeem yourself. After all, nobody's per-fect. Wait! Hold on a minute. That's one of the idiots we'll cover later in this book.

In reality, while some may differ, not *everyone* in the work-place is an idiot. Some organizations have more than others. Some companies import their idiots; other companies home grow theirs. I have never been at a company that didn't have at least a few. Now, on the flip-side, I have met and worked with some exceptional people. These folks are rare. When you do discover one, make them part of your work-circle. Not only will this help you in your career, it'll help you maintain your sanity. The average worker is neither an idiot nor exceptional. While you may strive to become exceptional, at the same time, you should avoid, at all cost, becoming an idiot. That's where this book comes in.

Forrest Gump's mother put it rather nicely, "Stupid is as stupid does". Being inept doesn't make you an idiot, it makes you inept. Being naive makes you naive, etc. The personality types I cover in these pages are "purposeful". By that, I mean deliberate in their thoughts and actions to cause harm. While idiots are few in number, they can cause great havoc.

Throughout the pages of this book, I do not name names, companies or individuals with whom I've consulted. Similar to the motion picture industry's disclaimer, "no idiots were harmed in the writing of this book". You, the reader, need to do your own identification. I've never relied upon someone else's label/opinion of another. You know the situation. You're new on the scene and, inevitably, on the first day, there is that one person who is telling you the be-all-and-end-all about everyone in the company. Do yourself a favor. Make your own assessment of people.

One example of labeling was when I first arrived at a major, private bank. As the *new guy*, I relieved the prior *new guy* assigned to a department which was headed by the "Dragon Lady". This had been going on for years. On my first day, after being informed of my *unfortunate luck* and how I was about to be *eaten alive*, I made my way to the eighteenth floor. Ms. "So-and-So", Executive Vice President, was actually far from being a "Dragon Lady". Yes, she was demanding and had high expectations, but rightly so. Her department made hundreds of millions of dollars for the bank. The systems her department relied upon needed to be functioning around-the-clock.

I earned her respect, where others had failed, by making sure her expectations were met. When the next *new guy* was hired, rather than relinquish the responsibility for the department, I maintained it. Over the coming years, Ms. "So-and-So" and I not only formed an excellent working relationship, we became good friends. The result was visibility to the CEO, CIO, and CFO which helped greatly when asking for and approving my yearly consulting rate increases, which were substantial.

The workplace is typically structured like an iceberg; one-seventh is above the surface, while the largest remaining mass is below the waterline. The portion above the surface represents management, both upper and middle. The portion below is the day-in, day-out workforce. Many people, over the course of their career, will span both sides. It's important that you learn even the most rudimentary navigational skills during your career to avoid getting sunk like the Titanic.

Idiots are not only in management. They are all around you; above, across the aisle, and beneath. I will provide examples of all three but let's start with the boss. Who hasn't had a Manager, Supervisor, or whatever their title, who *must* continuously, and I emphasize the word *must*, change, tweak, or improve (and I use that word *improve* lightly), everything you do? This boss never quite spells out what they want...and it's your fault for not being a mind reader.

SCENE: Somewhere in Corporate America...

BOSS: Fred, get in here. *(Fred enters the boss's office.)* Fred, I want you to put together a presentation that shows the advantage of a Popsicle having a stick at each end.

FRED: Are there any particu....?

BOSS: *(Cutting Fred off.)* Fred, I'm a busy man. You have your instructions, now go do it. And, I want it on my desk first thing in the morning. *(Fred exits.)*

The next morning...

BOSS: Fred, get in here. *(Fred enters.)* What part of our conversation yesterday didn't you understand?

FRED: *(Defensive.)* What's wrong? My presentation shows a Popsicle with a stick at each end and the advantage being that one can eat it like corn-on-the-cob.

BOSS: That's not the problem. What you failed to do was to make the sticks at each end round, light blue, and flared with a twist.

FRED: But when I tried to asked you if there were any particu…

BOSS: *(As usual, cutting Fred off.)* Never mind. If you want something done right, you've got to do it yourself.

The boss's last line is pure bullsh#t. These people never do anything themselves. Later in the day, the boss will instruct Fred to modify the presentation, find fault again, and repeat this back-and-forth nonsense until the idiot is finished abusing his authority and Fred is totally demoralized.

Let's examine this scenario a little deeper. Obviously, the boss set Fred up for failure. Idiots perform this ritual day-in and day-out in the workplace. It became quite evident on the morning after the task was assigned, that the boss had very particular requirements which he didn't share with Fred. Although Fred tried to elicit additional input, he allowed the boss to negate his attempts. Fred, therefore, contributed to his own demise. Lesson Learned: Don't allow yourself to be silenced. Reiterate what you understand the assignment to be, including the details you were provided. Specifically ask if there are any additional details you need to consider. Your goal is to make the boss provide greater clarity or confirm that you have the necessary information to succeed.

My advice: Once you return to your desk, detail the assignment in an email and send it immediately to your boss. Your email must explicitly ask for a confirmation. The subject line should read: PLEASE REVIEW & CONFIRM. Never forget: there's many a boss who didn't know what they didn't want until they didn't see what they didn't ask for. Got it?

I actually worked with a Vice President who asked for a spreadsheet providing a year-over-year analysis of my program's twenty-three million dollar budget. As I stated above, I asked all the questions, sent and received back confirmation on the request, and proceeded to complete the task. The next morning, this idiot asked why I didn't populate my numbers into an existing spreadsheet format he had already created. My answer was straight forward, "They would have been had you shared that little tidbit with me. But seeing that you didn't, you have my numbers, you have your spreadsheet, go for it."

Did you notice that, in the sub-title of this book, I used the word *"with"* and not *"for"*? There is a major distinction between those two words. The Merriam-Webster Dictionary defines them as follows: *With* – a participant in an action, transaction or arrangement; *For* – on behalf of, representing. I don't know about you, but I prefer to be an independent participant, not an idiot's representative. Working *with* someone conjures a partnership, a collaboration, shared responsibilities and shared successes. Working *for* someone conjures being a subordinate, unequal, and a lesser participant in the collaboration.

The word *for* is best used to describe those who hold elected office. The President, members of the House of Representatives, and the Senate are *supposed* to work *for* the people of the United States on our behalf, representing the will of the people. While this certainly is no longer the case, that's another book. Whenever someone asks who I work *for*, I always reply, "I work *with* so-and-so." You should be doing the same. Even out the playing field. Respect is earned and earned daily.

Now and then, you will encounter someone who has reached the *pinnacle of idiocy*. This person is known as a "total jackass". This personality disorder (and it is a disorder) thrives on your discomfort, purposely creating chaos and confusion where none existed prior to their arrival. The old joke goes: How many prima donnas does it take to change a light bulb? One! They simply hold the bulb in the socket while the world revolves around them. Make no mistake, these are dangerous people. They can change the atmosphere of the workplace as quickly and as devastatingly as a cyclone, leaving a path of destruction and debris strewn among the desks and filing cabinets.

The idiot above...

The total jackass personality specific to management is created primarily when someone has been elevated to a position of authority and possesses neither the smarts nor the necessary experience to fulfill the position. This personality is fed by a lack of self-confidence for which they over compensate by being unreasonable, rude, and in a perpetual state of self-misery. They prey on the weak and are belligerent to the strong who stand up to them. They embarrass people in front of others, easily lose their tempers, and can raise their voices inappropriately when remaining calm is what the situation calls for. The question everyone always asks themselves when they encounter this type of personality is:

"How did *this* person get *this* job?" Just like the perfect storm, it takes a careful orchestration of what initially appears as several unrelated factors combining to form the "beast".

Factor #1: Someone higher up made the call to promote this person. This could be for several reasons: the higher up is as inept as the person being promoted and couldn't recognize ability if it bit them on the "you-know-what"; the higher up purposely wants a pit-bull in the position because that's "just what the organization needs – a kick-in-the-pants"; while they, themselves, don't want to be directly responsible. By the way, a "kick-in-pants" never improved anything in the workplace. Many times, during my interviews, I am asked to perform that exact role, the pit-bull, to clean up a situation and get things back on track. Leaders are not pit-bulls. We'll cover leadership and management in greater detail in a later chapter.

Factor #2: The "wrong person at the wrong time" syndrome. This occurs quite often. As the higher-up goes higher, they often drag along their cronies and position them into jobs they are ill-prepared for. While the higher up may be very well-suited for his/her new position, it doesn't necessarily mean that those who worked under him/her at a lower level are suited for their new responsibilities.

Factor #3: The "I'm moving up...you're not" paper-chase quandary. You know these Managers. They have more initials after their names than the combined alphabets of English, Russian, and Chinese. It usually looks something like this:

Billy Bob Managuri, B.S., M.B.A., P.H.D., I.D.I.O.T., A.S.S.

Many have no real-world experience, only the world of academia. Now, before some of you become upset, this does *not* pertain to *everyone* who has earned advanced degrees. A number of people, who I have great respect for and who are in the "exceptional" category, have such degrees. But, they also have the work-and-life experiences that put education into practice. That's the difference. Unfortunately, too often in corporate America the quest to get graduates from "Ivy League" schools places too much responsibility too early in their careers. There is a proper way to indoctrinate a recent graduate, as our next story will illustrate.

Frank Wharton - M&M Mars Corporation...

I have been very fortunate to have had several extraordinary "business" mentors during my lifetime. Foremost was Frank Wharton, a retired, divisional President of the M&M Mars Corporation. Frank was the Chairman of the Board of Directors for two of my companies. Frank also enlisted other prominent corporate executives from other corporations to sit on my boards, as well. These gentlemen not only helped me, a young novice, learn and advance my education through the tried and true methods of "trial by fire" and the "school of hard knocks"; they provided the seed capital or services necessary to help launch these enterprises.

Whenever Frank would be in the New York City area, we would arrange to have dinner together. I always looked forward to those times since Frank would share with me stories about his business experiences. One story, in particular, was when, as a recent graduate of the Wharton School of Business with a degree in Industrial Engineering, Frank went to work for Forrest Mars (the son of Frank Mars, the Founder of the Mars Corporation). For those who may not be familiar with what an Industrial Engineer does, it's primarily process improvement; finding a better way to "skin-a-cat". Process improvements would result in cost reductions, improved time to market, and so forth. The very first thing Mr. Mars said to young Mr. Wharton was, "Before you can tell me how to improve my business, you need to know my business, from the ground up".

During his first two years at the company, Forrest Mars had Frank work in every department, from accounting to manufacturing, learning every aspect of the business. One day, Forrest approached Frank and said, "I'm sending you to Indiana. There's a situation I want you to take care of. One of our largest retailers will no longer purchase our products. The owner operates a chain of over one hundred stores in six states and has refused to even speak to one of our salesmen. You can come back when we know why our products aren't on their shelves, and not before".

When Frank arrived in Fort Wayne, he went immediately that morning, at eight o'clock sharp, to the home office of the store chain. Frank introduced himself to the receptionist and asked for an appointment to see the owner. Frank was immediately informed, in no uncertain terms, that the owner would not see him under any circumstances. Frank politely thanked the receptionist and then made himself comfortable in the waiting area; sitting there until closing.

Frank continued to do this same routine day-after-day; introducing himself to the receptionist, asking for an appointment, being refused, and then sitting for eight hours in the waiting area. After a week of the same repetition, Frank would leave the reception area for just a moment to get some breakfast at the corner diner. One morning, while seated in the diner, the receptionist rushed in and told him the owner wanted to see him. Frank and the receptionist dashed back to the building as fast as they could run.

Once inside the owner's office, Frank was asked to have a seat. The owner was impressed with Frank's perseverance and believed he earned an explanation. The owner went on to explain that there had been a problem with products going "bad" in the stores. When it was brought to the salesperson's attention, nothing was done about it. Basically, the stores were told that they would have to throw out the old and buy all new products. Frank listened very carefully. The owner showed Frank a ledger which reflected the monies lost across the chain and that it made no sense to continue to do business where the outcome was a losing proposition.

Frank, having a ground-up approach and the experience gained over the past two years, had an understanding others, in similar positions, didn't possess. Frank thanked the owner for meeting with him so that he could better understand the situation. Frank then informed the owner that the problem would be taken under serious consideration and that a solution would be forthcoming.

When Frank reported back the situation to Forrest Mars, along with a suggestion on how to rectify the problem; M&M Mars became the first candy company to introduce a freshness program with date stamping on their products. Going forward, it became the responsibility of the distributor to exchange new product for old that reached the expiration date. The solution was presented to the owner of the store chain. A trial period was established in half-a-dozen stores. Within six months, all one hundred stores had Mars products back on their shelves.

Years later, Frank was assigned to turn around a failing candy company based in England which the Mars Corporation had acquired. The troubled company was losing millions of dollars a year. Within a few years, the company was revamped and became highly profitable. Today, those products are still known as Skittles and Starburst.

People want to be happy, right? That's what we strive for. While balancing our work and home lives presents many challenges, it certainly doesn't help if you've allowed yourself to take on what you are not capable of handling. Two books by the authors, Dr. Lawrence J. Peter and Raymond Hull are recommended reading: The **Peter Principle** and the **Peter Prescription** (humorous treaties). The **Peter Principle** is a belief that in an organization where promotion is based on achievement, success, and merit, that organization's members will eventually be promoted *beyond their level of ability*. The principle is commonly phrased, "employees tend to rise to their level of incompetence".

The **Peter Prescription's** premise is simplistic; go back to a position where you were competent and happy. No one ever does. Have you ever known *anyone* who had themselves demoted? I doubt it. So, they remain incompetent and miserable.

Idiots and total jackasses will tell you what nice guys (or gals) they are; how nobody understands the pressures they're under, the enormous amount of responsibility they carry, and on and on. Don't be fooled. It's a ruse - the verbal equivalent of "slight-of-hand". They know instinctively that they are disliked, not respected, and have few allies. Perhaps they can persuade you into becoming one? This relationship will never turn out in your favor. The saying, "a leopard can't change its spots" rings true. These personality types will remain, regardless of how much sympathy they enlist from you and others, and will continue to make everyone's life miserable at work. Even worse, if when you arrive home after work, all you can talk about is what so-and-so did, had you do, reprimanded you for, etc., the idiot has achieved their ultimate goal; the ability to "affect" you 24 x 7. Don't despair. As we've shown with Fred and his boss, throughout the pages of this book, are examples for how to counter and survive.

The idiot across the aisle...

Let's talk a little about lateral idiots; those to the right-and-left of you. While these people don't manage you, they are integral to your success. You have your piece of the puzzle; they have theirs. But, at the end of the day, the pieces need to fit together. The common trait for lateral idiots is that they think they *are* your boss;

that it is their mandate to tell you what to do and how to do it. Quite often, they are not even competent fulfilling their own responsibilities, let alone directing yours.

One of my favorite examples was when I was engaged at a large, global pharmaceutical company. I had met with the CIO earlier the previous week where he expounded on his infrastructure vision for the company. While it was something never tried before, he asked me if I thought it was do-able. My reply was, "Absolutely." The truth be known, I had been experimenting with such an approach in my computer lab for the past year with excellent results, which is why I knew it could be accomplished.

Unbeknownst to me at the time I accepted the engagement, another consultant had been brought in months earlier to architect and implement the wiring closets and frame-relay worldwide. My "modeled" server-workstation approach would be dependent upon his effort. My first day on the job, I was working late into the evening. The only other souls around were the architect, we'll call him "Howie", and a desk-side support tech who we'll call "Gus".

SCENE: I was typing when I looked up and found Howie standing in my cube. Once he noticed I was looking at him, he immediately went into his spiel:

HOWIE: Let's get something understood. You only have responsibility, no accountability. I have the accountability to the man in the corner office. You, on the other hand, only have responsibility. My accountabil......

ME: *(Cutting Howie off.)* Howie, shut the f@#$ up and get out of my cube.

HOWIE: *(In total disbelief.)* Who do you think you're talking to?

ME: After hearing you speak earlier today about what it is you're doing and how you're doing it...plus your bullsh#t now, I'd say I'm talking to a f@#$'n jackass. And, if you don't get your ass out of my cube in three seconds, I'm going to stand up and throw you out.

HOWIE: We'll see about...

ME: One

HOWIE: You just try to...

ME: Two

HOWIE: *(Storming out of my cube, back to his and packed up his briefcase.)* You just wait 'till tomorrow. I'll fix you. *(Howie left.)*

I sat there chuckling and went back to my work. When I looked up, Gus, who had witnessed all of this, was now standing in my cube. He reached out and shook my hand vigorously.

GUS: *(With a big smile on his face.)* Thank you! We've been waiting six months for someone to do that!

ME: *(Smiling back.)* You're welcome.

The next morning when the CIO arrived, I was sitting at my desk, packed, and with my coat on. The CIO asked me if I was going somewhere. I replied that I would be if I were to have anything to do with that jackass, pointing to Howie's empty cube. The CIO smiled and said, "No". I proceeded to take my coat off. Needless to say, Howie didn't last long after that incident. On the CIO's behalf, I made a few phone calls and contracted AT&T to do the wiring closets and MCI for the frame-relay at half the cost, in half the time, and even more importantly, done right.

What finally did Howie "in" was of his own making. This is usually the case with idiots; they self-destruct. It's just a matter of time, and it certainly is in *everyone's best interest* if you can help to move up the timetable. Howie's day of reckoning came when we were having an internal, network audit. The CIO was traveling overseas and asked that I be the point-person for the exercise. The morning session with the auditors and the CIO on video conference went very well.

The afternoon session was another story. Both the CIO and I were being drilled on points of contention that would not normally be part of a routine audit. Something was amiss. After the session ended, I went back to my desk. Before I could even take my seat, the phone rang. It was the CIO. He had one question: "What happened between the morning and afternoon sessions?"

I told him Howie knew one of the auditor's wives and went out to lunch with them. There was a moment of silence. Then the CIO said very calmly, "Go down to my office, close the door, and wait for the phone to ring." I did as requested. When the phone rang, and before I could say "Hello", the CIO started: "I want him out of every system; revoke all access. I want his workstation confiscated. Tell the guards to shoot him on sight. I want that son-of-a-b#tch annihilated, wiped off the face of the earth! Understood?" I replied, "Consider it done."

The next morning when Howie entered the building, much to the CIO's dismay, the guards didn't shoot him. When they asked for his badge and laptop, he immediately went into a tyrannical fit, throwing both down onto the granite floor. The laptop was destroyed. Howie was escorted from the building, never to be seen or heard from again. The planets re-aligned, the seas calmed, and all was right with the world. Hallelujah!

You may have gathered by now that I don't take much bullsh#t. I never have and never will. I've worked very hard to be one of a handful of consultants who are the best at what we do. It may not be prudent for others to be so forth-right in handling such matters unless one is prepared to leave the job, should that be the solution. I always am.

Lateral idiots need to be put in their place. If you are not prepared to do it yourself, enlist your Manager. This is not a he-said-she-said bout. You must support your claim that the idiot is interfering with your ability to successfully complete your work. It must be substantiated by others. You never ask for a person's dismissal. You ask for another resource that has the qualifications to work with you as a replacement. In most cases, you already know who you would prefer to work with. Make the suggestion. A seasoned, good Manager already knows who's trouble within the organization. If the trouble does not fall directly under them, they can approach the Manager who does have that authority.

Should the situation not be rectified, document your work-effort and those situations when, how, and who has impeded your progress. A weekly status report summarizes this quite well. It's also an excellent way to provide your Manager with insight as to what you've been working on and what your accomplishments are (or have been).

I did this shortly after I started at the private bank I mentioned earlier. Our Manager, the VP of Networking, was a mainframe guy and had no idea what the new breed of network/system engineers did all day. The Manager never asked for a weekly status. This was my own doing. But once reviewed by the Manager, the status report was very well received. His initial comment was, "You do all those things? I had no idea." It was the first step in acquiring his respect. These are things you should be doing every day.

A large part of how I handle my everyday interaction with people stems from the education I gained working in a mental health facility. That extraordinary experience has benefited me every day of my life. Most days, I'm still dealing with the same personalities; the only difference being these people wear suits and have titles. There wasn't a single day at the facility that wouldn't bring insight to the complexity we call being human.

Each day, when I would arrive at the facility, I would go to the nursing station and read the charts of any new patients who may have been admitted overnight. One particular day, I read the chart of a man who had been acting up in a local bar and had been brought in by the police for observation. The chart stated that the patient had been a former prison inmate and had killed a man during his incarceration. The chart went on to state that the killing had been ruled self-defense. There weren't too many details, but the chart did emphasize not to mention his mother, as this would set him off.

I went to the unit and introduced myself. I informed the patient that every Monday, Wednesday, and Friday I supervise a group session with the patient community and, since today was Wednesday, he would be joining us and that participation was mandatory. It was about thirty minutes before the session was to begin. I told the patient I was going to get a cup of coffee in the kitchen and that he was welcome to join me.

SCENE: As we sat in the kitchen, the nurse entered and asked if I would mind her completing the assessment on the patient. I told her it was okay. The nurse proceeded to ask questions and filled in the answers as the patient replied. Then, the nurse asked him a question pertaining to his mother. I sat there watching. After a long pause, he answered. The nurse, having completed the assessment, thanked him and left. As the patient and I were walking back to the Community Center where I held my sessions, he started to make a low growling sound, stopped, turned, and looked at me intensely.

PATIENT: You know, I was gonna kill ya in the kitchen.

ME: *(Calmly.)* Really? Why?

PATIENT: Well, that nurse, ya know…she talked about my mother.

ME: So? She mentioned your mother, not me. Why were you going to kill me?

PATIENT: She's a girl, ya see…so I'd have to kill you!

ME: Well, that doesn't make any sense at all. But, you did manage to control yourself, and that's really the only choice you'll have while you're here.

PATIENT: I don't know…

ME: *(Moving one step towards him.)* I do. So, let's get something straight. You act up and I'll have you shipped off to a state institution so fast it'll make your head spin! Are we clear?

PATIENT: *(Dropping his feigned posturing.)* Yeah…

ME: Good!

What the good doctors taught me very early on during my tenure was that every patient, in some manner, will attempt to gain the upper hand. If that happens, you've lost control. It's imperative that you immediately recognize the *play* and address it. Bullies are notorious for intimidating others by acting aggressively or in a threatening manner but are cowards when confronted. Some other means of manipulating control are: helplessness, good looks, and pseudo-intelligence (talking above people's heads with babble which, upon scrutiny, would be the equivalence of a doctor telling you that the head bone is connected to the knee bone).

Don't allow fear to incapacitate you. Most people have a phobia or two. Perhaps you have a fear of spiders or snakes, heights, bridges or tunnels, swallowing pills, clowns, or the color blue (that one I made up…but you never know). Statistically, the number of people who have perished from a bridge or tunnel collapse is just about zilch, nada, squat. The same is true for swallowing a pill or going to the circus. Poisonous snake and spider bites are rare…and the majority of people, who are bitten, survive; unless you're in the Amazon. In that case, good luck.

What every phobia has in common is the fear of dying. So, there is only one fear, death. The point I'm making is you are at far greater risk tripping while walking, falling down a flight of stairs, or having a car accident, all of which could result in death. Yet, you do these activities every day. Think about it; then make yourself fearless.

At the same time, don't allow someone's helplessness or their beguiling to become your Waterloo. It's easy to recognize if you've been manipulated. Did you just do something that otherwise you normally wouldn't have? If you did, you've probably been manipulated. If a request makes you uncomfortable, don't commit yourself. Always allow some time to pass before you make a final decision. Don't confuse someone who needs help with a manipulator whose weapon is "helplessness". Study up on the signs of this passive-aggressive tactic. Sounds easy not to be "taken in", and most people think they never are, but there are some very, very cunning individuals who you will interact with over the course of your career (and during life, in general).

The same is true when dealing with pseudo-intellectuals. Under no circumstances should one ever let these idiots get away with their "babble". On more than one occasion, I've been known to come straight out and say, "What the hell are you talking about? Nobody understood a single thing you just said. Let's try it again, and this time, in English!" If someone is incapable of explaining *what it is they're doing* and *how they are doing it*, there is a major problem, which more-than-likely will, at some point, become *your* problem. This is never to be tolerated. This type of speech is a "cover-up" to the simple truth that they are inept and only serves to bamboozle their intended recipients. Your team and your initiative's success will greatly appreciate your effort to stop this nonsense.

You've heard the saying, "the face that launched a thousand ships". While it's been scientifically proven that attractive people are more likely to have things *go their way*, there is a distinction between a person who goes about their activities who just happens to be "good looking" and someone who uses their "good looks" to manipulate.

One day when I entered the mental health facility, sitting in the Community Center was the most attractive woman I had ever seen. Unbelievably stunning! Before I could reach the Nursing Station, she was up out of her chair and standing directly in my path with a seductive smile...a smile, I later learned, not only capable of launching a thousand ships, but sinking them, as well.

The woman introduced herself, touched me on my sleeve, and expressed her hope that we would have an opportunity to talk later in the day. I assured her that we would and continued on to the Nursing Station. Once inside, the unit Psychologist grinned and said, "Beautiful, isn't she?" Still in awe, I answered, "Yes... extremely!" The Psychologist then handed me a book and said three words, "Read, then assess." The subject of the book: Borderline Personality Disorders. In the weeks that followed, this woman's smile, gate, posing and the like, were more disruptive to the unit than the effect of all the other patients' disorders combined. Because of her attractiveness, I had to consistently remind myself of the reason why she was on the unit; she had a disorder, and my being manipulated wasn't going to help the situation. It was an amazing lesson in restraint.

The example above was not meant to infer that every good looking person has a disorder. Borderline personalities are not common. However, let's be honest, many good looking people do use their attractiveness to their advantage. While there is nothing wrong with that, it only poses a problem if you've allowed yourself to be manipulated. Just a word-to-the-wise, prior to committing oneself to anyone, regardless of their personality type, look before you leap; stand-up and speak-up for yourself. Be principled.

Bullies...

I won't tolerate idiots who attempt to use intimidation as their primary weapon of choice; not when I was a kid, and certainly not as an adult. As a kid, one incident happened when I was in junior high during gym class. As you came out of the locker room in your gym shorts, you took up a position on the volleyball court practicing until everyone was finally on the court. I hadn't been out on the floor for more than a few minutes when one of the much bigger kids came onto the court and immediately shoved me from my spot, informing me that *that was his position*. I immediately told him to f#$& off and put up my fist. He laughed and said, "You've got to be kidding?"

I approached him, but because of his additional height and reach, he grabbed me, took us to the floor, and held me down. I very calmly informed him that he had two choices: one was to get out of my spot; the other was to kill me. Because if he didn't get out of my spot or didn't kill me, once I was back up, I would keep coming at him, and coming at him and would never stop...never! He told me I was crazy. I answered I was and asked what his decision was going to be? He shook his head in disbelief, let me up, and got out of my spot.

Another example happened as a young adult when I started college. I was in my early twenties. I started later than most students as I had enlisted in the U.S. Army after high school. I also worked for several years after my tour-of-duty to squirrel-away more money before becoming a freshman. While taking a biology class over the summer, I got a job as a Security Guard at a major home improvement company. No, it wasn't Home Depot or Lowe's. They didn't exist then. My post was the back gate. From 1:00 p.m. until 9:00 p.m., I would check in and out tractor trailers either leaving or coming back to the warehouse.

SCENE: One day, about an hour into my shift, a limousine drove up to the gate. This was the first time that a vehicle outside of a tractor trailer had ever appeared. I walked up to the driver-side window, exchanged papers; walked to the front of the vehicle and wrote down the license plate number; walked back to the guard shack and opened the gate. Five minutes later, the phone rang. It was the Chief of Security, a former U.S. Marine and U.S. Secret Service agent; shaven head and all.

ME: Hello, back gate.

CHIEF: You f%$#in son-of-a-b#tch! That was the f$#@in Chairman of the f$#@in Board and you had a f%$#in cigarette dangling from your f%$#in mouth you...

ME: *(Cutting the Chief off.)* Whoa, whoa. Now, do you hear me cursing at you?

CHIEF: *(A steady-stream of profanities.)* %$#@ &^%$ ^%$#

ME: *(Again cutting the Chief off.)* Oh my God, you better get someone out here quick!

CHIEF: *(Concerned.)* Why? What's wrong?

ME: *(Very calmly.)* There's nobody watching the gate. *CLICK*

I got into my car, drove to my apartment complex, put on my swimsuit, and went down to the pool. I wasn't going to take that crap for a b-flat job that paid minimum wage. The next day, I found another b-flat job that helped to pay the bills.

The idiot below...

"Look out below" should be the battle cry when dealing with idiots beneath your level in an organization's hierarchy. Don't mistake someone who has yet to reach a level of competence (a novice still learning the ropes) with someone who's an "interference".

Primarily, this personality shows itself when a co-worker is convinced that they were *undeservedly* passed over for a promotion, award, etc. Recognition they believed they rightly deserved. I am not going to validate the legitimacy of such a complaint. For all I know, the complaint might or might not be true (experience has taught me that it is usually the latter). It is the response that is the root of the problem.

Does anyone truly believe that poor behavior is the best means to rectify such a situation? Typically, an attitude such as "I'll show them" manifests itself; spiraling out of control until a pink slip, rather than a certificate of commendation, is what they are handed. Signs of someone who has fallen into this category include: excessive complaining, gossiping, bad-mouthing fellow co-workers, inappropriate language, an "I could care less attitude", arriving late / leaving early, substandard workmanship, etc.

I can sympathize with someone who was truly deserving of recognition and was passed over. I can't sympathize with someone who allowed such circumstances to cause them to self-destruct; ruining their own career and impeding the success of others. Whenever I witness such destructive behavior in a member of my team, I take it upon myself to see if I can help.

Recently, a young engineer, whose work-effort was exemplary, started to wane (showing the signs stated above). I took him aside and asked if there was a problem. There was. He had asked for an increase in his hourly consulting rate and had been "flatly" denied and because of this, was seeking opportunities elsewhere. I didn't want to lose such a valuable member; it takes considerable effort on the part of a Leader to cultivate a "team" and even the loss of a single member can have a rippling effect.

I was very familiar with the agency he was under contract with. It was commonly known that this particular agency underpaid their consultants and kept margins for themselves as high as forty percent. Despicable!   On his behalf, I called the agency and negotiated a rate increase with two options. I then took the young man aside and detailed his two options and their respective pros and cons. Option two was selected and implemented and the engineer's work-effort reverted back to his previous level of excellence and a potential problem was averted.

There have been countless times I've interceded on behalf of my team members in "righting a wrong". On the other hand, if a team member has a misconception that they were *deserving* when they were not, I set the record straight with them. At that point, they have two choices; get back to reality, knuckle down and demonstrate that they are deserving of reward at some future time; or pack-up and move on from the team. I always provide people some leeway to self-correct, but you won't find me holding my breath. I don't look good in blue.

When a co-worker is finally out of the picture, either through a dismissal or of their own volition, it is rather easy to categorize that co-worker's former contribution to the organization. If you and your colleagues will truly miss seeing this person in the days ahead, they were an asset. If everyone smiles, waves, and mimics Vanna White saying, "Bye-bye", the co-worker was an idiot. If, on the other hand, the entire department turns out for a party and sings, "Ding dong the witch is dead", a total jackass has left the building.

How many idiots does it take to change a light bulb?

None! They never see the light.

Chapter Two – "It Was a Very Good Year"

When I was seventeen, it was a very good year.

Several of my friends asked that I include a biographical chapter to give readers some insight regarding my formative years. As I stated in the Author's Note introduction: *who you are...is who you are.* Very seldom is there any distinction between how one conducts themselves at home and at work. Your family, upbringing, environment, life experiences and circumstances combine to form your personality...for good or bad.

I was born in Paterson, New Jersey; the son of Joseph and Enes Glaeser. My father was of German decent and my mother, Italian. If there had been a little Japanese somewhere in the family, I could have been the Axis Powers. At the age of seven, my father purchased a newly constructed home in a small, private lake community called Sparta Lake, in Sparta, New Jersey. My father's purchase practically happened overnight. Just a few days earlier, my older brother had been playing stick-ball in the street and almost got hit by a car. That weekend, my father headed for the country; found something he liked, and bought it. That summer, we moved to the top of the mountain overlooking the lake.

From that moment on, I was hooked on swimming, fishing, hiking, camping, ice skating, and sleigh riding. I couldn't spend enough time outdoors (I haven't changed). I played baseball, football, and hockey. My grades in school were above average, but I didn't study much and seldom did homework. I was fortunate to love reading and had excellent comprehension skills and the ability to memorize almost instantly. I made friends easily and effortlessly crossed the boundaries between different "cliques" in school.

My senior year, I was class President, was on the Executive Committee of the Student Council, and was also the President of the Teen Association at my lake. All in all, I had a great child-hood. No complaints, no regrets. That was largely due to my parents, a few exceptional teachers, and a few extraordinary adults in the community; coaches, businessmen, etc.

My childhood idols were many; both real and fictional: Jim Thorpe, All American (the single, greatest athlete that ever lived); Beethoven and Tchaikovsky, Mickey Mantle, Batman, The Lone Ranger, and so on. I was always a little odd in the sense that I was very focused; my sister thinks I was born in a suit jacket and tie. Each Christmas, particular gifts were repeatedly requested: a science kit – one year biology, the next year chemistry, followed by geology, meteorology, and so on; two record albums: one classical, one percussion; a sports related item: a baseball mitt, a football, or something for my fishing tackle box; and last, but not least, books...all sorts of books. From the Hardy Boys series when I was young, up to the complete set of the Harvard Classics as a teen.

I'm going to take a moment here to digress in the interest of education. The Harvard Classics comprise a 51-volume anthology of classic works from world literature, compiled and edited by then Harvard University President, Charles W. Eliot, and first published in 1909. The collection of literature ranges from Plato to the lectures series, covering the fields of history, poetry, natural science, philosophy, biography, prose fiction, criticism and the essay, education, political science, drama, travelogues, and religion. The set was claimed to constitute a reading course unparalleled in comprehensiveness and authority; what every educated man should have knowledge of with respect to a liberal arts program. The Harvard Classics are still available today. The cost ranges from new, for fifteen hundred dollars, to used, between three and five hundred dollars. If you or members of your family love to read, you may want to consider obtaining a set.

My first theatrical production was in Kindergarten. I had the role of a spinning top. While the constant twirling made me nauseous, and the costume made me claustrophobic, I was hooked...applause, when combined with the smell of greasepaint, can be quite addictive. In fourth grade, I wrote, produced, and performed in my first original play. While I can't recall the storyline, I do recall that it was unfinished, and yet I still convinced Mrs. Richter to allow us to perform it for the class.

I think she realized after an hour that we were just "winging it" and called a halt to the production. It wouldn't be the first time that the curtain went up and down, and a show closed on the same day. Such is life in the theater.

Over the years, I did many productions with high schools, colleges, and community theater groups in various roles; director, actor, musical director, author, producer, etc. I have gone on to write two award-winning plays and am currently writing a comedy with Broadway as its ultimate destination (you must have goals). I have read parts of the play to close friends, and they've found it quite funny. That and three fifty will get you a cup of coffee at Starbucks. What translates from paper to stage and then stage to audience can be quite a surprise.

After high school, I enlisted in the U.S. Army and served three years on activity duty and then three years inactive reserves. Throughout this book are stories from my service. This is one of my favorites. Our little group of eight was always getting into trouble on the weekends while in training. My buddies and I, while we were Army, were stationed at the Naval Amphibious Base at Little Creek, Virginia. Our antics were harmless; stupid little things like sleeping on the sand in Virginia Beach, which is a "no, no", or a "slightly inebriated" soldier taking a pee on a cop car, while the two cops were still sitting in it; nothing of a felony nature; just young men letting off steam.

What transpired was always the same; the police would turn us over to the Shore Patrol (the Navy's equivalent of the Army's Military Police), the Shore Patrol would turn us over to the MPs, and the MPs would escort us back to base and wake up our Commanding Officer; usually around three or four in the morning. Our Commander would come out, usually in a tee-shirt and boxer shorts, chew the hell out of us, threaten severe reprisals for getting him up in the middle of the night, and then go back to bed. By Monday, it was usually forgotten and nothing ever came about it with regard to punishment.

But, there was this one time when the Commander was calling us into his office, one by one. I think it was the time we had a slight altercation with a group of Marines in a bar; or as we put it, a gentlemen's disagreement. When it came to my turn, the Commander started with, "Now, son." I immediately interjected, "Don't call me son, you're not half the man my father is." Do I really need to go on? I guess I should. Well, as you can probably imagine, that didn't sit too well with the Commander. As I recall, I think my punishment lasted until the very last day of training. Still to this day, I can peel a potato faster than anyone I know.

Years later, when I left the service and came home, my father pulled out a letter. It was from my Commanding Officer. The letter went on to tell my father about the incident in his office and what I said. He told my father how he hoped that when his newborn son grew up, that his son would have the same love and respect for him as I had for my father. He went on to tell my father how my training was going and that I was a good soldier and that he would be proud of me. The letter ended with him asking my father not to share what he wrote until after I was discharged. My father kept that promise. Dad told that story often over the years. It was great to see him smile.

I remember the first week I was home after being honorably discharged, it was early Spring. I was sitting in Krogh's Tavern in Sparta, New Jersey, having a drink when Mr. Dimmick walked in and sat next to me. I had gone to school with his three sons. Mr. Dimmick asked me what I was up to. I told him I just got out of the Army. He asked me if I had a job yet. I said no, as I had only been back home for a few days. His immediate response was, "Let's not waste time here. You be at Sussex Industries first thing tomorrow morning at eight o'clock sharp! You're working for me."

Mr. Dimmick was a retired engineer and had purchased a small machine shop in town. I think he did this to keep himself occupied and not fall prey to wasting away, as many retirees do. I was soon to learn that every conceivable odd job was Mr. Dimmick's and Sussex Industries' forte. One week I'd be climbing smoke stacks testing for air pollution for the State of New Jersey, the next week building dog houses, and the following week sandblasting an Olympic size swimming pool. Every day was an adventure. There was no doubt that I earned every penny I was paid.

When summer was almost over, a friend of mine asked me if I would be interested in managing the car wash in town. Her father owned the business and her boyfriend, who was managing it, was heading back to college. Sounded like a good deal. I accepted. Mr. Dimmick was sorry to see his best worker (his only worker) move on. But he understood. As fate would have it, just as the following Spring approached and I was about to lose my job to the returning boyfriend, another friend came to see me and told me "Harry" needed to talk with me right away, it was important!

"Harry" was Harry Coder, a former Decca/MCA record executive who lived in town and opened up Sparta Records. A small shop primarily carrying top 40 albums and 45's, had an excellent classical selection, an assortment of accessories, and catered to special orders for everything else. I grew up hanging out in the record shop whenever Mom would go downtown. Mom would drop me off and then go do whatever a Mom did at the supermarket, pharmacy, bakery, etc.

I learned almost everything about music from Harry; the classics, jazz, the big bands, country and western, rock 'n roll. You name it. I was also an exceptional drummer; having studied first in the Sparta school system and then with the American Percussion Ensemble. I knew Harry had been ill for a while. On my last visit, a young woman who helped out in the shop was now managing the place during Harry's absences.

Now that Harry was back, there was trouble. The young woman had no ear, no business sense, and had purchased whatever a salesman told her to buy. The shop was filled with inventory that could never sell. Harry's shop was in serious, financial trouble. Harry asked if I would take over and manage the shop. He was still recovering and would only be able to visit now and then, but knew in his heart and soul, as he put it, that I could turn things around. Harry also knew from my friend that I had plans to attend college in the Fall. Harry understood that I would be sacrificing school, but needed someone he could trust. I told Harry not to worry. College could wait.

As an added incentive to the base salary offered, Harry had two tickets, every Friday night in my name, at any Broadway show of my choosing. I saw every musical, drama, and comedy that lit Broadway for almost two years running. Great memories!

At the record shop, funds were limited, so I needed to spend Harry's money wisely. The bad thing was, being a small shop; the distributors wouldn't take back inventory for cash, credit, or trade. I was stuck with what was in the shop. Each day when a different salesman would stop in, they'd push whatever new releases they represented. I'd spin up a record, listen, and either place an order or listen to the next. One day, after listening to a new release, I told the salesman to put me down for five-hundred 45's. He asked me if I was serious. He thought the song was "crap!" Absolutely, five-hundred 45's, I repeated. I sold every record and had to order more before long. The song was, **Seasons in the Sun**, by Terry Jacks. Yes, the song was "crap" as the salesman put it, but I knew it would sell.

Another song I did the same thing on was, **The Night Chicago Died**, by Paper Lace. Over the next few years, I had an amazing track record of picking winners. Record sales and "accounting for people's taste" have nothing to do with each other. They still don't! The advantage to picking winners was that our shop had the record in inventory while others did not. By the time other stores would get up to speed, our inventory would be sold and the fad would have passed; leaving them with unsold inventory and us with cash.

While moves like this helped, they weren't going to resolve the disastrous inventory problem the former clerk had created. Fortunately, I had met the Store Manager of a large record store chain a year earlier at a party. The chain operated thirty-eight stores from Massachusetts to Washington, D.C. His store was located in the biggest mall in New Jersey and did millions in sales annually. I paid him a visit. My pitch was straight forward. I told him, unlike my mom-and-pop shop, no label or distributor was going to say "No" to him when retuning merchandise for credit. I suggested an exchange. I would swap the "bad inventory" in the shop for top 40 merchandise, dollar-for-dollar. He would be able to return my "bad inventory" for full credit and re-inventory top 40 merchandise back into his store. The result, I would have merchandise that was sellable. He agreed.

Over several months, little-by-little, the swaps occurred, sales improved significantly, and so did the shop's bottom line. After almost two years, Harry was now financially in excellent shape; however, not health wise. His health had continued to deteriorate. One day, Harry told me he had an offer for the shop. He would be glad to discount the price and hold the note if I was interested in owning the store. I told him I very much appreciated his offer but needed to get out into the world and start college. Harry smiled and told me he knew that would be my answer. He said he always saw something in me that was going places.

A month later, Harry sold the shop. On my way to California

to start school, I swung by Harry's home to say goodbye. Harry thanked me for helping him out and then handed me an envelope. When I opened it, there was a cashier's check made out to me for twenty-five thousand dollars. When I protested, Harry said it was the least he could do. He had more money than he could spend in the time he had left and wanted to make sure I got off to a good start after postponing my plans and putting my life on hold while I helped him out. I thanked him. That was the last time I saw Harry. While I spoke with him a few times while I was at college over the next year, I hadn't taken any trips back East. One night my phone rang. It was Mom. Harry had passed away. I often think back to those wonderful times. I miss my friend.

During college, I had some interesting jobs. My first was as a phone solicitor for the Sun Telegram Newspaper. This was a suggestion from my brother. I distinctly remember telling him, "I can't do that!" The thought frightened the hell out of me, but I went on the interview. That's a laugh. Any warm body that walked through the door was hired. The first night, I was handed a script. It read so stoic, I would have hung up on myself if I was on the other end of the phone. When I finished, I crumpled it up, through it in the waste basket, picked up the phone, dialed, and made my first call; "Hello, this is Doug Edwards, calling on behalf of the Lend a Hand Foundation. Are you currently receiving the Sun Telegram Newspaper?"

Yes, I didn't use my real name. I got the gist of what to say from the script and reworked it in my mind. The premise was simple. One, mention the charitable organization up front; two, see if they are already a subscriber. If they were, thank them, hang up and go on to the next call. If they weren't, give them the pitch. Three, if they said they weren't interested, thank them, hang up and go on to the next call. But if they went, "ahh" or "ooh", they were mine! I was closing seven to nine sales a night; a record! Within two weeks, I was room Manager; helping others and getting an override on their sales. It was a numbers game, as well as speaking to the person at the other end of the call exactly as they spoke. If they sounded like a truck driver, I was a truck driver. If they were flirtatious, I flirted back.

The money wasn't bad, but it wasn't enough. Although I had the G.I. Bill to help out, the cost of an apartment, furniture rentals, car payments, insurance, food, tuition, books, etc., required more than I could make sitting on a phone each night for three hours. Harry's money was tucked away for the future, and I had no intention of living off of it. Fortunately, opportunities always presented themselves. The largest operator of adult book stores in San Bernardino County needed a new money runner. The job paid three hundred dollars a week, excellent money back then; especially for a part-time job.

The job was simple. Visit each store and pick up the cash receipts for the day. Bring the cash receipts to the company's headquarters, wait for it to be counted, and then placed in night deposit bags. Then, take the bags to the bank and make the night deposit. All total, about three hours work a night; the same as the phone job, but at twice the money.

A few months into the job, I began to feel as if someone was watching me. I mentioned this to the owner. His response? He gave me a cattle prod to carry with me. Then one night, about six months into the job, as I was leaving the night deposit slot, two men, dressed in suits and overcoats, approached. I was just about to zap them with my cattle prod when they reached into their coats and pulled out their identification: FBI. They began to ask me all sorts of questions. All I could tell them was exactly what it was I did. I picked up the cash receipts which were already bagged, brought it to headquarters, waited, and then took the night deposit to the bank. That's it. Like Sergeant Schultz from Hogan's Heroes, "I know nothing!"

The next night, when I brought the cash receipts to head-quarters, I mentioned my unexpected visit by the FBI. The owner laughed and said everyone gets that visit and not to worry. Regardless, I was not comfortable and tendered my resignation. I knew I wouldn't look good in stripes; especially when they ran horizontally.

The same week that I retired from *a life of crime*, I was per-forming with the college jazz band. One of the band members brought me to the attention of a new artist who had recently been signed to the Capital Record label. He was looking for a new drummer. The band member thought I'd be great for the job and arranged for the artist and me to meet. To be quite frank, I really wasn't all that interested in playing in a band outside of the jazz band at college. I had done the club circuit; rock bands, soul bands, etc. and would rather concentrate on my studies.

Besides, my drums were back East. I explained all this to the artist who simply asked for me to "just think about it" and that he would be back in touch. Two days later, he called and asked me to come over to his house. When I arrived, in his living room was a new drum set, cymbals, hardware, and all. He told me I now had no excuse that my drums were back East. I like people who are creative and go the extra mile to make things happen. He reminded me of myself. I joined the band. That "in" lead to other contacts and gigs. While going to school, I made the money I needed to live on doing studio work and going "on the road" for new artists for both the Capital and Warner Bros. labels.

Life on the road was good. During the day, the band would be put up at a nice hotel while the artist would be at a few local radio stations plugging their song. The rest of us would be lounging around the pool. At night, the band would perform at a local club so that the locals could come out and meet the artist. Sometimes we would be in town for a day or two, sometimes for a few weeks. There were always the afterhours parties back at the hotel lasting until sunrise. The parties always ended with the locals heading for work and the band going to bed. But inevitably, we'd be "on the road again."

Funny, we never seemed to travel in a straight line; always bouncing from one state to another. One week we'd be in Albuquerque, New Mexico and then have to travel up to Boise, Idaho. I came to learn that the booking agent who planned the tours had a nick-name; it was "Dart Board Sam." You get the idea. Unfortunately, none of the "new" artists I performed for made it big; while their songs and performances were as good as and sometimes better than some that did make it. It's a tough business. Most people don't realize the huge investment of capital the record labels make to discover that one artist who connects with the public. When you're young, this is a great life, but I didn't see myself doing this for a living until I was an old man. Like the lyric in **West Side Story**, "something's coming." I just didn't know what.

I went into the field of computers not by design, but by fate. A friend of mine was the head of systems for a worldwide fragrance company. One evening, while having dinner with him and his wife, he told me that there was a new invention, it was called the PC, and it was going to take over the world. He said that someone needed to learn these "new-fangled contraptions", and it was going to be me. "Why me?" I asked. "Trust me," he answered. "You'll see." With his help, I bought my first computer. The cost was a little over five thousand dollars. The amazing thing is that the watch I wear today is more powerful than that first computer. My friend provided me with some books on programming, and I was off and running.

Periodically, my friend would visit, look over my shoulder, and critique my progress. Patience wasn't his strong suit. Now and then, he would whack the back of my head, remove me from my seat, take over the keyboard, and correct my code. For almost a year, I worked at the computer every day writing code. Then, one day, my friend, instead of whacking my head, commented, "Well, you've made it. You're dangerous now." It was a new beginning...and my friend was right; I was cut out for this. The machine and I got along extremely well.

While most of my computer associates were coding for video stores, hair salons, and the like; I saw the market as saturated and not very profitable. I did a little research and discovered a niche. The first programs I coded were for small to mid-size trucking companies. Back then, the only trucking software available was mainframe based and had a huge price tag to match. The only companies that could afford the cost were the "giants" of the trucking industry. I changed that.

Many of you may be familiar with the first step prior to writing code is requirements gathering. You can't code until you know what it is you're supposed to be delivering. So, for the next month, I practically lived at the trucking company working in every department; accounting, warehousing, dispatching, and even going on the road with a few drivers. Once I knew the business inside-out, and the owner's take on how he wanted his business to operate, I was ready to hit the keyboard.

One day while working with the dispatcher, a very gruff and scary looking man walked into the building and headed straight into the owner's office. When he emerged a short time later, he walked up to me and said in a growl, "You're mine, next!", and left the building. I went to the owner's office and asked, "Who the hell was that?" It turned out to be a friend of his who owns and operates a salvage yard. Seemed the man had a problem that he wanted a piece of software to resolve. A week after I finished up with the trucking company, I went to see Ace at his salvage yard.

The problem was unique. Ace didn't sell auto parts, as most salvage yards would do as their primary source of revenue. Rather, Ace separated the vehicles into sixteen commodities; e.g. steel, rubber, aluminum, copper, etc. These commodities were stock-piled until the market was just right to sell. The problem was Ace had no idea what he had in inventory at any given point in time.

A few months later, after completing my code and integrating my application into the weigh station system, we "kicked off" step one. For the next month, all vehicles brought into the yard were chopped and maintained in separate piles. At the end of the month, step two was implemented. The sixteen commodities were loaded onto trucks and weighed individually. The weight of each commodity was divided by the number of vehicles recorded for the month. Now we had an average weight per commodity per vehicle. I took those calculations and applied them to my code. Once implemented, Ace had a "real time" indication of what was stock-piled in the yard. When a commodity was sold, it would weigh-out and be subtracted from the inventory totals tracked in the system.

I should tell you that the biggest challenge wasn't getting my system to work; it was trying not to be eaten alive by the dozen *junk yard dogs* who would greet me every time I arrived. While Ace was a shrewd businessman, he was quite a character. One day when I walked into the office, hanging on the wall above his desk was a new picture. It was an aerial photo of a combination gas station and food service complex. I asked Ace what was up with the picture. Ace went on to tell me that "him and the boys" stopped at this "same damn place every damn time" they headed down and back on their frequent trips to Florida. He was tired of always having to pay for his gas and food, "So, I bought the damn place!" Another day when I arrived, a U.S. Army tank was parked in front of the building. When I asked Ace, "What's up with the tank"? He replied, "I always wanted one; thought it be fun." Later that afternoon, I watched from the weigh station as Ace rode around the yard demolishing everything in sight. Then, there was the one time I had to stop at his house for some reason or other. When I walked into his living room, parked in the middle of the floor was the biggest, most awesome Harley-

Davidson motorcycle I'd ever seen. Once again I had to ask, "Ace, what's up with the bike in the living room"? Ace just smiled and said, "Ain't she a beauty? I like lookin' at it. Can't do that if it's parked outside all the time."

He might have been a little eccentric, but he always treated me with respect and was generous. The week before Christmas, as Ace and I were walking back to the office building from the weigh station, he asked me what he owed me for the week. When I told him, he reached into his pocket, took out a wad of cash, counted it out, and handed it to me. When I counted it, there was five hundred dollars more than I had told him. I brought this to Ace's attention. He looked at me and answered, "Why, that's your *damn* Christmas bonus. Merry Christmas!"

While the money was good writing software, it wasn't long before I realized I didn't want to be sitting behind a keyboard all day, day-after-day, writing code. My only regret was I was going to miss *"those damn dogs"*.

I started scanning the help-wanted section of several newspapers each week to see what the next "emerging technology" was based on demand. Networks started to surface. So, I taught myself the two networking systems that were prevalent at the time; Banyan Vines and Novell, and became a certified Network / Systems Engineer. Next came Distributed Systems; the capability to remotely touch and deploy to servers and workstations from a central location. So, I learned Tivoli, CA UniCenter, and SMS, the preferred systems. I continued to build my computer consulting practice, always staying ahead of what was coming next; always leading edge. This is not an easy thing to do.

Over the years, I have spent hundreds of thousands of dollars maintaining my computer lab to learn new technologies, and have invested thousands of man-hours, off-the-books, teaching myself the intricacies. But, it paid off, as I have done very well for myself. Today, I am no longer a full-time "propeller head". Rather, I now specialize in recovery; resurrecting failed initiatives. As a Senior Management Consultant, I head up large, IT portfolios and programs for Fortune 500 companies. It's worth noting that, as much as I enjoy what I'm doing, on the day that I do retire, the first person who mentions that they have a computer problem had better run for their life.

Politics and religion can be touchy subjects. So, let's get

touchy. I was raised Roman Catholic. I had two uncles who were priests and two aunts who were nuns on my father's side of the family. One particular Sunday, my uncles were grilling me on that day's sermon.

My father stepped in and pretty much told them to "Knock it off! Keep it up, and he'll just stop going all together." In fact, when my brother, sister, and I turned thirteen, after receiving Confirmation, you had the choice whether you wanted to continue going to church or not. My brother and sister opted out. I didn't. It wasn't so much of a religious thing as it was spending time with my Dad.

I believe in God. Perhaps you don't. For me, I have personally witnessed both miracles in my life, as well as having come face-to-face with evil. If you haven't experienced this for yourself, no amount of my writing could convince you to become a believer. I have people say to me, "Well, what about Adam and Eve, the apple and their being banished from Paradise and original sin...you believe that really happened?" The answer is "Yes." But the story is allegorical. After all, you and I are here. So, at some point, there had to be the creation of the first man and woman. That's indisputable. This does not take away from evolution, which is a scientific fact. But, the "spark of life" is unexplainable for me by any other means than the creation of life by God. Adam and Eve weren't banished because they ate an apple, but because they took of the *tree of knowledge;* that knowledge was the moment when man and woman became aware of their own existence; their consciousness. It was this knowledge, the knowledge of our mortality that resulted in paradise being lost and was original sin. No other life on earth lives with this knowledge, this dichotomy.

Then, there are those people who point out, "But Jesus gave up on God when he was on the cross." I'd reply, "Are you referring to when Jesus said, "Why hast thou forsaken me?" My understanding from what I've read and learned from theologians was that at that moment, Jesus took upon his soul all the sins of mankind that ever were and ever would be. It is inconceivable to fathom the pain and agony of this act of mercy by Jesus. Although Jesus was the Son of God, to fulfill His mission on earth, the Father had to sacrifice His only Son so that we would know the way to the Father through the Son.

These words were spoken that we might believe in Him and might emulate His faith and confidence in God's deliverance, even in the most terrible of circumstances.

I try to live my life the best I can. I've made mistakes. There have been those times I've hurt others. I have been asked to forgive and have asked for forgiveness for my own transgressions, as well. We all know the saying, "life is short." I don't hold grudges. I move on. At the same time, I don't allow someone to make their problems, my problems. Hopefully, part of me will go on through those I've helped during my lifetime. That's all anyone can ask for.

Politics is, by and large, the most controversial topic. So, here goes. I am a conservative and a traditionalist. I believe in doing for oneself and making your own way in life; no handouts. I never had any and was never interested in either pursuing or receiving any. The cold, hard truth is that very few people have an actual need for assistance. Those who fall into this less-than-one-percent of the populace deserve to be helped and are helped. It is the larger percentage of those on the government "teat" who are milking the system, that I take issue with. And when I say government, I mean local, county, state, and federal institutions. These people are just lazy; pure and simple.

My sister has chronic Crohn's disease. She was in her mid-twenties when she became ill; young for this disease. At that time, no one had even heard of Crohn's, and we almost lost her. After months of battling the disease, long hospital stays, one doctor finally figured it out. Through medication and diet, she recovered. However, over the years, there have been times when she'll suffer a flare-up, causing her to become hospitalized and bedridden for a considerable amount of time. Yet, for as legitimate as my sister's illness is, she has never been able to receive one nickel in government assistance during these critical times.

Rather, it is my wife and I that cover the rent, car and other payments until she recovers and is able to go back to work. To make it even more frustrating, the news reported on a woman who knows how to play the system, who isn't ill, and receives the equivalent of eighty-five thousand dollars a year in government assistance. If anyone condones this absolute absurd abuse of our tax dollars, they need to have their head examined.

"One-percenters" are now being portrayed as evil people; that we somehow miraculously fell into money and want to inflict hardship upon the masses. Bullsh#t! I work an average twelve-hour work-day and have put in many sixteen hour days when it's come down to "crunch time." My commute can be up to three hours each way to get to and from the job. I earned every penny I've made and have paid all the taxes required. But to some, this isn't enough; they think that I haven't paid my fair share. As for all the hype about loopholes and write-offs, that's bogus.

When my mother became ill, I moved Mom from Pennsylvania to an assisted living facility in New Jersey. This was so that I could put her under the care of my doctor (whom I trust) and to be able to see to it that she had a quality of life for her remaining time. With the proper care being administered, we were blessed to have my Mom around with us for another two and a half years. I also had the added blessing of seeing her almost every day, as I would stop by on my way home from work to visit. On the weekends, I would pick Mom up and have her spend time with us at the house or take her someplace fun for the day.

The money spent was inconsequential. The only thing that mattered was letting this woman, who raised me so well, know she was loved. The point here is, not one single penny of this cost could be written off my taxes. Not that that mattered. I wasn't looking for a write-off. But, you'd think that our government would place children caring for their parents as a top consideration. It isn't. The government we currently have in place views the elderly as a burden; and shares a similar attitude with Scrooge before his reformation, "Then they better die quick and decrease the surplus population."

Countless people are writing on these topics today; the collapse of the family; the doing away with long standing traditions; zealots incorporating political correctness into every aspect of our society. Thousands and thousands of new laws introduced each year at the city, state, and federal levels, controlling more and more of our lives; from what we can eat and drink to confiscating our property. The majority of folks are not paying attention; and that's the problem. I fear for the future of this country if its citizens don't wake up and reverse the downward spiral into the abyss.

More and more people in our society are becoming government dependent and living off the hard work of others. A few years back, there was an email circulating of a college professor who ran an experiment with his class to help illustrate the downside to such a socialistic approach. Whether or not this experiment was actually implemented is not relevant. What is interesting is the premise.

An economics professor at Texas Tech stated he had never before failed a *single student* but had, once, failed an *entire class*. The class had insisted that socialism worked. With socialism, no one would be poor and no one would be rich, the great equalizer. The professor then told his students, "Okay, our class will have an experiment on socialism. Starting this week, all test scores will be averaged and everyone will receive the same grade. No student will receive a failing grade on a test and no student will receive an A." After the first test, the grades were averaged and the entire class received a B. The students who studied hard were upset and the students who studied little were happy. But, as the second test approached, the students who studied only a little, studied even less and the students who had previously studied hard decided they wanted a free ride too; so they hardly studied at all.

After the second test scores were averaged, the entire class received a grade of D. Now, none of the students were happy. A week later, when the third test results were complied, the test scores once again averaged out to a D. For the remainder of the semester, the average test score on subsequent tests never rose above a D. The students bickered, name called, and blamed each other for not studying and bringing the score higher. Finally, at the end of the semester, the entire class ended up failing the course, much to their surprise. The professor then pointed out that socialism would ultimately fail, as the experiment had demonstrated. In a capitalistic society, the more an individual applies them self to succeed, the greater the reward. But, in a socialistic society where government takes all the rewards away, no one will even try or eventually succeed. Remember what Margret Thatcher, the former Prime Minister of England, said, "Socialism only works until the other guy runs out of money".

I'll be one of the first to admit that I can be stubborn. I'm a Taurus (not that I'm into Astrology); but nothing like I was when I was younger. Over the years, I have learned to "let go." When I was twelve and my brother was fifteen, we were having a wrestling match with our Dad on the living room rug. When my Dad got my brother into a no-win situation and suggested that he say, "Uncle", my brother immediately complied and was released. When my

Dad got me into the same position, I refused to say "Uncle". He twisted a little more. Again, I refused to say "Uncle". My Mom, who was sitting on the couch watching, gently said to my Dad, "Joe, you might as well give up. You'll snap his arm off before he'll ever give in." She was right.

Dad gave up and released me from the *death grip* – it should be noted that fathers always make up names like the *death grip* when wrestling with their siblings. Now, I don't want anyone calling DYFS. First, Dad would never hurt us; it was play. Second, DYFS would have a hard time contacting him; Dad passed away back in 1999. And, about me being stubborn…over time, it morphed into tenaciousness. How's that for a transformation? I don't think my wife is buying it.

As the Professor in the **Wizard of Oz** said to the Tin Man, "A heart is not measured by how much you love but how much you are loved by others". My wife and I very much enjoy entertaining and having friends and family over to our home often. Helping people I've worked with and then formed a friendship with has always been important to me. Four times during the warmer months (May-August), my wife and I host a "get together" for these friends. It's not an easy list to get on. And no, we are not snobs. The group just happens to be particular. There are several membership requirements: one, you can't be an idiot; two, you are a warm, caring person, and three, you laugh at my jokes. The third requirement being the most important!

I have consulted at some companies where more than one person has been extended an invitation to join our group and some companies where not a single person made the grade. These "get togethers" are great fun and a great opportunity for everyone to help each other if someone is in need of a new opportunity, advice, or a place to vent their frustrations. The invitation always extends to wives, husbands, a significant other, or a friend, and everyone arrives with an appetizer, a side dish, or a dessert. I always supply the meat. I'm very particular about what goes on my grill.

It is my sincerest hope to meet readers of my book, in the coming years, that will be joining us. Don't forget your swim-suit. The pool is kept at eighty-eight and the spa is at one hundred and one.

Chapter Three – "Back Stabbers"

What they do! They smile in your face, all the time they want to take your place.

There are countless personality types you'll deal with over the years. They may or may not be idiots; that depends on how extreme their quirks are. These personality types can range from just being a pain-in-the-ass all the way up to a total jackass. Keep in mind that the workplace is typically not the medium that bred these personalities. The workplace is, however, a Petri dish full of nutrients to grow and embolden a few without the constraints of outside influences to keep them in check. For me, it makes no difference if someone is a man, a woman or a visitor from another planet. A co-worker is a co-worker. I interact with everyone identically.

Let's review some of the more common types you're bound to meet, if you haven't already. Please note: Personality types can and often do cross over creating what I've coined, the "combonality". When taken to the extreme, bits-and-pieces taken from each type, the "Frankenstein Monster" is born. It's not a myth. While extremely rare, they do exist. I've met a few from time to time. Should you meet one yourself, my only advice is...run for your life!

When some of my friends learned I was writing this book, their immediate response was, "Am I in it?" Jokingly, I'd reply, "No...the sub-title of *that* book would be, **Idiots I've Known,** and it would be a multi-volume set."

****

The "Mother Hen": For all their self-righteousness, Mother Hens have been known to lay their share of eggs. Typically, this is a female employee who has been with the company for what seems like an eternity - (there is no sexism intended here, it's simply a fact).

Age is not a factor. Not all Mother Hens are old. Some started with the company when they were very young and could be your age or even younger. They know everyone and have worked in various departments over their many years at the firm. They are extremely protective and territorial. In fact, so much so that they'll incubate their chicks to the point that they don't hatch, they explode. Their outer demeanor is "sugar and spice and everything nice".

Be careful. They will never cooperate where change is concerned. Anything that will uproot their traditional and sacred ways is met with resistance. Their distain will not manifest itself with anger or be confrontational in any way. That's where the sweetness comes in. They will talk in a syrupy manner, never raising their voice, and always with a *pasted* smile and repeat, day-after-day-after-day, how things are done at the company. They will wear you out. The average person will eventually just give up. Mother Hen, one, everyone else, zero.

You can reverse the scoreboard to read, Mother Hen, zero. The solution is simple. You "yes" a Mother Hen. Yes to everything, then do exactly what you intended to do. This will eventually drive a Mother Hen crazy. Be prepared for a lot of clucking. When they remind you that you didn't follow the *rules*, there is another simple answer. It's, "I'm sorry, I didn't know". You continually do everything as you deem necessary, regardless of Mother Hen's constant reminders. There's the old saying, "It's easier to receive forgiveness than it is to get permission". Of course, if your methods prove to be a failure, you'll have some explaining to do.

One last point on this subject; always be willing to at least listen to what is being suggested. I never stated that you should totally disregard *everything* that is being said. Now and then, there will be a gem. This reminds me of a story my father told me when I was young (who'd have thought).

After serving in the Navy during World War II, my father installed linoleum floors during the day and went to school at night to become a Mechanical Engineer. Upon graduating, he went to work for a small tool and die company. He started with three other recent graduates who were all told that they were on a probationary period. After six months, one would be selected to stay on with the company. Each day, during lunch, one particular "old timer" would share stories about the job with the newbie's. At first, the stories were new and interesting but, after some time, became old. Often, the "old timer" would repeat himself. One by one, the other three newbies drifted off until only my father was having lunch with him. I asked my father why he would keep listening.

Smiling, my father replied, "Yes, he certainly did repeat himself a lot, but everyday he'd say at least one thing he didn't say before...something important. His stories helped me to become a better engineer, and I was grateful." At the end of the probationary period, my father was selected and stayed with the company for almost forty years until his retirement. My father was an amazing Dad, man, and engineer.

The lesson my father taught me was simple. Whenever you think you've heard it all before, that you think you have all the answers, keep your mouth shut and listen. If you listen at least twice as much as you speak, you'll learn something. Even a "Mother Hen" will serve you well every now and then if you listen.

The male counterpart of a Mother Hen is known as a "Pa Kettle". Please note, they are *nothing* like a Mother Hen. Although, they too, like Mother Hen, have been around forever, Pa Kettles don't give a damn. You can do anything you want. They could care less. They are just biding their time until the day they can retire. Pa Kettles are grumpy, cantankerous and gruff. They could choose to make your life miserable if they wanted to, but they're too busy checking their 401k, Social Security benefits, health plan options and the like to get involved with something as insignificant as you. As long as you do not interfere or impede in any way whatsoever, a Pa Kettle's retirement plans, you're gold. Never forget that or else you could wake a sleeping giant.

How many Mother Hens does it take to change a light bulb? Seriously, we're talking Mother Hen here…..."Careful now!" "Don't screw it in too tight." "Use two hands." "It's going in crooked." "Make sure it's a 40-watt bulb." Give up yet?

****

The "Barbarian": The worst of the worst. I have more distain for this personality type than any other and have absolutely zero respect for them. They are rude, obnoxious, arrogant, abrasive, condescending, uncooperative, conceited, domineering, pompous, belittling, smug...I could keep going, but you get the picture. They can change the atmosphere from congenial to hostile in an instant. And, they take advantage of every opportunity to perform that very act, especially in group settings, e.g. status meetings, phone conferences, etc.

Picture a conference room with a dozen people sitting around the table chatting, laughing, and socializing with each other during the few minutes before the facilitator brings the meeting to order. The Barbarian enters. A hush comes over the room. The meeting begins. As the facilitator goes over the meeting's agenda, one of the members politely asks if the team could go around the table and introduce themselves since two new members had recently joined. The facilitator agrees and asks the member who made the suggestion to go first. In typical fashion, each member gives a brief blurb on who they are and what they do.

Then it's the Barbarian's turn. Without hesitation, the Barbarian states, emphatically, that they will not introduce them self; that everyone knows who they are and what they do. The Barbarian spends more time reiterating why they won't cooperate than the time it would have taken to complete the harmless task of an introduction. The facilitator, in an attempt to dispel the hostility that now permeates the conference room, jokingly says, "Come on, I work with you and even I don't know what you do". The attempt fails.

The next member to introduce them self is the Barbarian's Manager. They, too, are aloof, barely saying five words. As the business of the meeting continues, the Barbarian is on the attack. They state that another member didn't follow through on a request from the last meeting (which the other member had accomplished). They constantly interrupt and inappropriately challenge other members while they are speaking. The meeting has taken on an atmosphere of gloom. As the facilitator looks about the room, each member's face has lost the initial enthusiasm they entered the conference room with. The facilitator goes through the rest of the meeting's agenda as quickly as possible and wraps up. The Barbarian, as they usually do, is up out of their chair and heading for the door before the meeting is officially concluded. They're off to create havoc elsewhere. That is their sole purpose in life. I can guarantee it follows them out the door when they leave the office at night. As Mr. "T" said, "I pity the fool".

Did you take note that during the conference room introductions, I portrayed the Barbarian's Manager as acting aloof? I purposely made mention of that fact for a very specific reason; Barbarism is a contagion. While most personality types are self-contained; Barbarism is highly infectious, and spreads readily from one person to another who is in close proximity; i.e. Managers and staff. There is no "magic pill" to counter this affliction. Be on guard and keep your immune system strong or else you, too, could succumb to this disease.

Let's study this scenario a little deeper. First, let's cover the creation of a Barbarian. What is a Barbarian? An individual referenced to be a brutal, cruel, warlike, insensitive person. This personality type is systematic of one who, earlier on in life, no one paid attention to. Barbarians have an acute case of self-doubt and insecurity. In order to get the attention they craved, at one point they discovered just how to achieve their goal...by being obnoxious. It worked. They became the center of attention, even if for all the wrong reasons. There is only one way to extinguish this personality type, they must be shunned (persistently avoided, ignored, and rejected). Under no circumstances are you to be confrontational. This will get you nowhere and will only serve to feed the "beast".

Ignoring and not "giving in" to a Barbarian's poor behavior will eventually pay off. While it may take weeks or even months, a Barbarian will, sooner or later, come to realize that their *attention getting tactics* are not having the desired effect. If they can't shake things up, what's the sense in continuing to be uncooperative? In other words, "the thrill is gone". This will become evident when the Barbarian begins to show their vulnerability; usually presented via a pleasant hallway conversation; showing up to meetings on time; being less aggressive. When this happens, it is the perfect opportunity to have that long, overdue one-on-one. What is it, outside of being a pain-in-the-ass that they contribute to the team, the organization? We never said that Barbarians were stupid. It's time to help them to redirect their energy and focus on how to achieve the attention they so desperately need. Cooperation, not confrontation; consideration, not contention, is the right direction. If done properly, one can actually turn a Barbarian into one of the organization's greatest assets. Give it a try. We can always use another ally.

How many Barbarians does it take to change a light bulb? What's a light bulb? Barbarians preceded the Dark Ages.

****

The "Full Steamer": As Scotty would invariably say in almost every Star Trek episode, "Captain, I don't think the engines can take much more!" Captain Kirk is the classic example of a Full Steamer. On a side note: Have you ever taken a train ride from New York to Florida without having a berth (a built-in bed or bunk)? Trust me, don't do it. Unfortunately, I did...*once*. I have a new slogan for the rail system: All are bored! And while we're on the topic of trains, it should be noted that Full Steamers have a total disregard for what lies ahead on the tracks. It could be Pauline, tied to the tracks waiting on her hero; a pile of timbers placed there by the James Gang. It doesn't matter, just shovel the coal.

Who doesn't want things to be completed in a timely manner? Well, quite frankly, a lot of people, such as those personality types we've covered and those yet to be covered in this book. So, you can understand the Full Steamer's dilemma. But throwing caution to the wind can, and, in most cases, will have disastrous results. So, how do you achieve the desired results and apply the brakes on a Full Steamer? It's not all that difficult if the Full Steamer is a peer. But, it's quite a different story if the Full Steamer is at the executive level.

What I've done in those situations is to send an email to the executive, with a few (and I mean a few), salient bullet-points specific to what the "hold up" is or was, and how the team mitigated or is mitigating such circumstances. Then, purposely not waiting for an email reply, I follow-up with an office "drive-by" (stopping in unexpectedly), to get their response as quickly as possible. At one particular company, I was brought in to recover a costly and complex situation that had been lacking any momentum for over six months. The executive was anxious now that I was on-board to "get things moving". While it had only been a few weeks since I took on the problem, I began to hear through the grapevine that the executive believed things weren't progressing fast enough. This was a potential problem I didn't need...sabotage via rumor and innuendo. This needed to be nipped in the bud.

First, I composed my email. Second, I made sure the executive was in his office, his door was open, and that he wasn't on the phone (all without being seen). Third, I then sent my email. Then, a few minutes later, I swung by his office and poked my head in and asked if he had a chance to review my email. He replied that he had (and if he hadn't, I would have suggested that now might be a good time). I told him I just stopped by to see if he wanted to discuss the situation or slap me upside the head. After he laughed, he invited me into his office, and we proceeded to have an open, frank discussion on the issues. Once he was made aware of all the roadblocks and hurdles that had never been addressed by the prior management and that those obstacles needed *first* consideration and remediation, the team was now finally in a position to move forward.

The executive appreciated the candidness and expressed his appreciation and thanks. He also expressed that while our conversation bought the team some leeway, since the program was "back-on-track", he expected to see the needle move favorably *very soon*; once a Full Steamer always a Full Steamer. I assured him it would, and it did. Full Steamers need to be met head-on; otherwise, crossed signals will result in a major derailment, all of which could be avoided with a simple, preemptive, factual-based conversation. Never implement a cover-up. While full disclosure and transparency may result in a few "lumps", it is the only way to earn respect.

How many Full Steamers does it take to change a light bulb? It's never a requirement. They travel at the speed of light.

****

The "Dribs 'n Drabber": If you ever hope to elicit a response from these people, you had better plan on attending Dental School first, because it is going to be like pulling teeth. Imagine filling up a five-gallon bucket one drip at a time...drip...drip...drip... drip...drip...drip...drip...drip...drip...drip...drip...drip...drip... drip...drip...drip...drip...drip. Annoying, isn't it?

Dribs 'n Drabbers relish in the fact that they can drive you crazy. It's hard to decipher what created this personality type. It's not that they're procrastinators. It's not that they're antagonistic. So, what caused this unique character to manifest itself? The best I can conclude is that this disorder is akin to being a miser; much like Ebenezer Scrooge, the information they possess is pure "gold" and must not be shared with others. A blatant "Bah Humbug" is sarcastically imbedded in every one of their email responses. To make matters worse, you need a cipher to translate the encrypted message hidden within their communications. It's like CIA training was a prerequisite before joining the company.

To prove the effect of a Dribs 'n Drabber with respect to the space-time continuum (as defined by Einstein's theory of General Relativity); I ran a simple experiment. I placed three Dribs 'n Drabbers in a confined, windowless room. In as little as one hour, I was rewarded for my effort. My staff and I actually witnessed the hands of a clock going backwards.

When you bring to a Dribs 'n Drabber's attention the simple truth that their cooperation is less than stellar, they play dumb. Often, they will retort with, "Relax, keep your pants on, what's the rush?" Eventually, the request will be accomplished and done right. However, the battle to bring closure will have drained everyone's patience. One way to address such stress is to allow a period of time to pass between requests. Such an approach would allow everyone's strength to be replenished. That would not be my choice.

Rather, I do just the opposite; I inundate a Dribs 'n Drabber with requests; asking for status updates; assigning new tasks; sending meeting invites, and so on. This tactic will have a similar effect to one that has been portrayed in countless sci-fi movies where a renegade computer system needs to be destroyed. You know the scene; the idea is to make the computer system go into overload mode, until it's spewing smoke and system shuts down. The hero gives the computer two directives in contradiction to each other. A conflict within the silicon pathways ensues and eventually destroys the evil, maniacal brain.

Once accomplished, you can then re-program the system to perform as it was intended to; by providing a benefit, not an obstruction. This is not an easy task, and many people do not have the skills or experience to re-program this unique personality type. A word of caution; this is best left to a professional (a seasoned Manager) or else one could find themselves in a similar situation to that in the movie, **2001 – a Space Odyssey**; where HAL (the on-board computer system) sets one of the astronauts, who was attempting to shut him down, adrift into deep space; never to be heard from again.

Many Dribs 'n Drabbers are highly intelligent. However, intelligence is not an excuse for being obnoxious, flippant or rude. This personality also has the misconception that they aren't accountable to anyone or anything. Those who act this way aren't as brilliant as they think they are and will only lead to making themselves *unapproachable*. That's just *dumb*! Unfortunately, many brilliant people behave this way. They believe its part of the mystic; their inherent right to be difficult.

Early in my career, when I was a "propeller-head" (highly technical), I found the solutions to many problems others were not capable of solving. This was a gift; an innate ability to see beyond the obvious and determine the root cause. I never acted superior. I wasn't performing voodoo or casting a magical spell to remain cloaked in secrecy. Rather, I would take the time to explain what the cause of the problem was, and how I went about resolving it so that others would learn. I made myself approachable. In return, I became the "go to person" and was given greater responsibilities, oversight, and leadership positions. My career took off.

Remember, being brilliant doesn't always equate to being smart or even being employed for that matter. It should be noted that the largest segment of the population who are unemployed are "geniuses". You will never earn the respect of others if you, yourself, are disrespectful.

How many Dribs 'n Drabbers does it take to change a light bulb? It's scientifically impossible! Dribs 'n Drabbers are the black-holes of the workforce; a spinning vortex where even the simplest request gets sucked in and can never escape.

****

The "Victor / Victoria" Syndrome: Are you familiar with the play or movie of the same name? A female posing as a man who, in turn, is posing as a female impersonator. Talk about an identity crisis. I had a debate with myself whether or not I should include this personality type. But, then I remembered telling myself that I was going to be totally honest and not leave out a personality that is troublesome just because it may be gender specific. After all, you need to be forewarned if you are to survive. With all the other personalities I covered until this one, I could find humor. This one, I can't. This is evil incarnate.

Female employees who display this disorder are bitter, vindictive, and spiteful. My personal belief is that it is centered on *transference*; the direct association of feelings for one person transferred to another. While the initial association is based on an actual relationship, the secondary association is not. The person at the receiving end of the transfer is usually unaware and undeserving of the ill feelings heaped upon them. For this reason, it is extremely difficult to correct the situation; especially when you are confronted by an "imaginary perception". The unfortunate recipient might be perceived as, "that bast#rd of a husband", the "boyfriend who left me", or some other dysfunctional relationship from the transferee's present or past life.

This is a "no win" situation. And, the transference is not just relegated to men. This personality type is an equal opportunity idiot; projecting their absurd thinking onto women just as easily. After all, other women might be "that b#tch who stole my husband". They live in a world of deep-rooted mistrust and conjure fantasies of revenge.

Since they have an identity crisis, a woman with a persona of a man who impersonates a woman, their snake-like demeanor is constantly "puffed up" to make themselves more intimidating to others. "*Who* said *you* could do *that*?" "*Well*, we're *just* going to have to bring you *back* into the fold." If Victor / Victoria should be in a position of authority or have the ear of someone who is, very few people, if any, will answer back for fear of reprisal. However, there are a few, such as myself, who will not tolerate such behavior. We are the *unintimidated*, driving this personality absolutely nuts!

They want an even playing field, to be accepted in the sandbox and be in the "big leagues" but, when challenged and don't get their way, cry, "He was *mean* to me". And, then they run off to anyone who will listen to report the catastrophic mayhem, existing only in their own mind, and supported only by rumor and innuendo, no facts.

The sad truth is, in almost every situation I have witnessed this phenomenon, the woman is a divorcee. They seldom smile and can barely utter an acknowledgement to your "Hello" as you pass them in the hallway. Even if you are only remotely a student of observation, you've witnessed it yourself. Think about it.

Please note: This personality disorder is not associated with every woman who happens to be divorced. Being divorced has nothing to do with the disorder's manifestation; that was only an outcrop. The problem is with the individual person and their coping mechanism. The strong survive. The weak become self-pitying victims bent on getting even. Unfortunately, it is the innocent who will suffer their wrath and misguided thinking.

This personality type is extremely unhappy and feels powerless outside of the office. And, for that very reason, given even the slightest bit of authority, has them expecting everyone to "kiss their butt". When their misguided importance of themselves isn't catered to, an internal rage sets in; then comes the scheming and, eventually, the axe. They will enlist other females who share a similar distain for anyone who thwarts their controlling nature. And, again, should they be in a position of authority, they live under the false impression that their position *demands* the respect of others. Nothing could be more wrong. Respect is earned and earned each and every day, one day at a time.

As I stated before, this is a "no win" situation. There is no way to combat someone bent on your destruction, even if their ammunition is pure fiction. Accept it and move on. Your only satisfaction should be, "What goes around comes around". I am a true believer in Karma. I have witnessed its effects first-hand. There *will* come a day when the evil that was done will come back ten-fold. As "Sarge" on **NYPD Blue** would say to his police officers before they'd hit the streets, "Be careful out there!"

How many Victor / Victoria's does it take to change a light bulb? If you're one of the lucky few, you'll be long gone before the bulb ever needs changing.

****

The "Class Clown": In classic Greek theater, the portrayal of comedy and drama were represented by the iconic laughing and frowning masks. The Class Clown perpetually wears the former. This idiot projects everything as a joke, but in reality, they know otherwise. They don the mask of the clown to deflect and hide their inadequacies from others. And, for that reason, it's almost impossible to get a straight answer from them. One of my steadfast rules: You are *not* allowed to be funny unless you are *proficient*...period.

Humor is key to making work enjoyable. And for that very reason, I've devoted an entire chapter on this topic later in the book. But, interjecting "funny" routinely is a deflection and fools no one; making it hard to take a Class Clown seriously. Now, when the time comes where a Class Clown needs to enlist the support of others...who's having the last laugh? Horseplay, practical jokes, and off-colored remarks at work are not funny. This isn't high school or college. Perhaps this personality type pursued the wrong "vocation" and would have been better off joining the circus when it came into town.

But, they didn't. And, you know this for a fact because the clown just entered your meeting spewing their latest stand-up routine: "Howdy folks! A funny thing happened to me on my way to the meeting. I made it! (Rump-bum) No, seriously folks, what'd ya call two people who put their heads together? I haven't a clue since I've never been asked! (Rump-bum) It's been a lot of fun. You've been a great audience. Don't forget, I'll be performing here all week. So, be sure to come back."

I've actually had clowns enter a conference room in a similar fashion and completely disrupt a meeting that was in progress. And, when you give them "the look", they come back with: "What?" "What'd I do?" "Oh, I'm sorry!" "What were you saying?" It's time to give this performer *the hook*. Most Class Clowns have a lot of smarts. What they don't have a lot of is self-confidence. If you are going to get anywhere with them, you have to be completely upfront. It's time for a little chat.

There are several similarities which people who lack confidence have in common: an inability to admit their mistakes, a fear of criticism, not willing to take risks, and needing the approval of others as validation of whether they performed well. The "how to" to reverse these and other self-defeating "confidence killers" cannot be covered in the span of this book.

It's a journey which requires a serious commitment of time and energy to accomplish. One can only help a Class Clown to recognize their deficiencies and encourage them to take the first step. Their journey will take them down a path covering their accomplishments and failures, their strengths and weaknesses, as well as establishing goals and how to achieve them. Helping a team member who's in need of help is never a laughing matter. It is everyone's responsibility to help, whenever possible.

How many Class Clowns does it take to change a light bulb? One...with a caveat; as a practical joke, they will have replaced the bulb with a black light, keeping everyone in the dark.

****

The "Contender": "Ladies and Gentlemen, welcome to Madison Square Garden. Are we ready to rumble? Tonight's bout pits "Just-for-the-heck-of-it" against "Can't-you-ever-just-agree". This is a twelve-round battle of wits ending in a draw. If you say "go right", they say "go left". If you say "go up", they say "go down". Everything is the opposite. Not that it is, they just think it's fun to play Devil's Advocate. "Someone has to look at things from the other side." No, they don't! Not if it's just for the sake of argument.

What warped sense of humor during man's creation brought about the antagonistic personality? The Contender can be extremely dangerous. Their goal is divisiveness through deception. They are very wily people and use many subtle methods to mask their real intent; primarily to make *you look bad* and to make *them look good*. Humor and flattery are not uncommon tactics in their bag of tricks to inflict harm. Contenders are masters of manipulation and illusion.

How does one go about delivering a "knock-out" punch that'll put this personality to the canvas and down for the count? You'll need to be cautious. While you might fight fairly, Contenders are known to fight dirty and will hit below the belt. My next piece of advice may sound self-defeating but, as your trainer, you've got to trust me on this; you must allow the Contender to push you up against the ropes. This is the tactic Muhammad Ali used to defeat George Foreman; known throughout the world of boxing as the "rope-a-dope".

A Contender can only be defeated by using their own strategy against them; deception. At first, allowing your opponent to pummel you doesn't look too smart, but the "rope-a-dope" maneuver has its advantages. For every question they put to you, you counter by refusing to answer and immediately counter by jabbing their own question back in their face.

Another technique is to let it be known, via the grapevine, an approach or position which you favor; while in reality, you actually favor the *exact opposite*. When the Contender makes it known, publicly, that they favor a position in opposition to the one you circulated, you simply counter by agreeing with them. A solid right-cross is impossible to block. The Contender will never have seen it coming. As you rise in the ranks from feather-weight to middle-weight to heavy-weight, there can be no greater confirmation than having management declare you the undisputed champion.

Now, on the flipside, playing Devil's Advocate has its benefits. I've been known to play this role with my team occasionally; not to rile anyone up, but to help them to focus. Have they thought everything through? Probably not. It's very easy to get caught up in the *big picture* and quite another thing to get down *in the weeds*. My punching holes in their approach or position teaches them to develop a defense; to be detailed, focused, to weigh the pros and cons, and to be able to substantiate their claims. A good Manager or Leader will do their sparring with his or her team members in a private ring; not in public.

How many Contenders does it take to change a light bulb? When you turn on the light to see if it needs replacing, they turn it off. You turn it back on, they turn it back off. You, on. Them, off. On, off. On, off. Just forget it!

****

The "Intimidator": In our feature movie presentation this evening, Arnold Schwarzenegger delivers the chilling line "Watch you're bach." Intimidators love to hold an employee's job security over their heads like a guillotine. Displease them and it's "off with their head!" This personality type constantly challenges and never rewards. They like to play bad cop and love to interrogate. Like the banditos in **Blazing Saddles**, Intimidators proudly declare, "We don't need no stinking badges".

A large percentage of people who report to this personality type will never *step up to the plate* for them. In fact, it's quite the opposite. People will do as little as possible to squeak by. After all, the more one does, the more there is to be challenged and left open to criticism and ridicule. Keeping a low profile is essential to one's survival. Don't confuse a Manager who sets high expectations with an Intimidator. This personality type purposely raises the bar to an "unachievable height" to make people feel uncomfortable. They get an adrenaline rush from using their power to affect and afflict.

This is one of the more difficult personality types when it comes to giving advice on how to counter because it's "damned if you do, damned if you don't." If one chooses to stand-up for oneself, it can easily escalate into being confrontational. If one chooses not to address the situation, one's work-life can be in a perpetual state of fear; never knowing *if and when* the axe will fall. Their deranged way of thinking has Intimidators purposely baiting others to *sound off.*

One of the most notorious Intimidators I ever worked with actually said to me in his office, "You're not afraid of me, are you"? I responded with, "Why the hell should I be afraid of you! When you're on the same playing field with me, then we'll have something to talk about". If you're an employee, I don't recommend that you handle the situation as I had. It could be construed as insubordination and lead to your dismissal. My telling him off actually earned his respect. His warped way of thinking needed to be challenged before he'd consider me an equal. This is not as uncommon as you might think with this personality type.

How should you handle such a dilemma? My recommendation would be as follows: If you are competent, if you consistently deliver and, if you have no intention of ever finding a new position within your present company which is outside of the Intimidator's control or leaving for a new company entirely, then you are going to have to have that one-on-one. The tactic is to force the Intimidator into acknowledging your worth to both *them* and the *organization.*

Start out by asking if they could give you some of their time. You would very much appreciate their advice. Once behind closed doors, come straight-out and ask if there has been a problem with your performance, your work ethic, or anything else you may not be aware of. If you've been performing, what else can be said except good things? Should the Intimidator bring up a legitimate issue or anything they believe that needs improving, it's always best to find that out as soon as possible so you can correct the situation. Thank them. Also, ask for ways that could improve communications between the two of you going forward.

This alternate approach is the gentler way to accomplishing what my straight-up approach accomplished; by gaining their respect. Once the relationship has solidified, future conversations will be the perfect opportunity to offer any suggestions you may have, as well as pointing out (very gently) a flaw or two in the Intimidator's armor. The majority of Intimidators will back off and be much less "in your face" after having a one-on-one and subsequent talks. If not, you've done all that you can do to earn their respect…it's time to look elsewhere for a job.

You never know when a situation could pop up that might cause feelings of intimidation. I was taking a few days off from work and was relaxing by the pool when my cell phone rang. The call was from the senior finance representative for the Information Technology Group who we'll call "Bob". A few weeks earlier, I had been asked by senior management to take over a failed program. The program's financials were a mess, a monumental mess. The corporate CFO wasn't happy. Are they ever? I take my financial obligations very seriously and was in the process of reconciling the books. The CFO wanted to review some concerns he had specific to this program.

Bob told me that, although he knew I was taking some vacation days, the CFO wanted a meeting that Friday. Since I was home, the meeting could be accomplished via a conference call. I told Bob, "No way!" If the CFO wanted to meet, I would come to his office for a face-to-face. Bob told me I was a "brave man". I replied, "Do me a favor, when I get there, make sure you have a cigarette and blindfold ready".

If I was going to face a firing squad, there was, "no way" I was going to do that over the phone. If I'm going to be shot, you're going to have to look me in the eyes when you do it (forget the blindfold). I spent the next two days of my vacation crunching numbers and putting together a presentation for the meeting. Friday morning, I met Bob in his office, and we walked down to the CFO's office together. The three of us sat around the small conference table and reviewed the numbers, the CFO's concerns, and my plan for reconciling the financial situation. There wasn't any contention or hostilities; just a frank discussion. The meeting concluded with the CFO stating that he had a better understanding of how the mess was created in the first place and was onboard with my approach to reconcile. As I was walking out his door, his last remark was, "Doug, thanks for coming in. I know you were on vacation. Appreciated!" I replied, "You're welcome", and headed home.

I could have been intimidated. But why would I be? If you are performing to the best of your abilities, you never have to live in fear of what others think or apologize for your workmanship. In fact, my coming in to the office fostered the CFO having a newfound respect for me. Never allow yourself to be intimidated. As stated before, stand-up and speak-up for yourself. Be principled. These are the moments that will set you apart from others and define who you are.

One last piece of advice...always be on guard. There is a potential for weak individuals to succumb to a diabolically phenomenon known as the Helsinki Syndrome. It occurs in individuals who are taken hostage by the job and held captive for long durations while the boss demands more and more loyalty. Diagnosed as a complex reaction to a very frightening situation; the disorder eventually develops into the captive having positive feelings toward their captor, the Intimidator. If your boss begins to resemble someone with a phallic helmet, large black cape, and a breathy, baritone voice; you've gone to the "dark side".

How many Intimidators does it take to change a light bulb? Bulbs never need replacing. "Intimidators" purposely keep the lights off since they know that many fear the dark, using this knowledge to their tactical advantage.

****

The "Yodelayheehoo": No, it's not a Ricola cough drop commercial. It's an idiot scaling the heights of Corporate America on the backs of others. This personality type is utterly ruthless and has no regard for the claw marks left on their victims. Taking any opportunity to take the credit for someone else's effort is their trademark. In fact, they will purposely orchestrate such opportunities. I have little use for this idiot and so should everyone else. I have never backed down from righting this wrong when it's been brought to my attention; I actually relish the chance to expose idiots like this and have done so on many occasions.

It is your responsibility to promote yourself; to take credit where credit is due and to see to it that people in a position of authority know your accomplishments. This is not "bragging". This is self-promotion and is absolutely necessary if you are to get anywhere in life. Don't be like the tree which fell in the forest which no one heard simply because no one was there to listen. Make some noise! And, make sure it's within ear-shot of people who can advance your career.

The best way to gain recognition is to take on the seemingly impossible and then successfully deliver. At every company, there are a multitude of tasks that repeatedly fail. These issues, over time, become the *"I guess we'll just have to live with them"* problems. If you have the smarts and the foresight to tackle and remediate these problems, you will become "gold" in the eyes of those with the authority to provide advancement. Again, make sure it is known that it is *you* who is taking on these Herculean efforts; not your boss, not a co-worker...*you!*

Once accomplished, do not, I repeat, do not share the "good news" with anyone else in the hopes that they will share with those in authority. You must handle all communications yourself, even if you have been instructed otherwise by your Manager. Trust me, I've never known anyone to be fired for directly informing the senior leadership that they resolved one of the company's biggest headaches and didn't give their Manager an opportunity to put their own spin on it.

I know first-hand that this is *do-able* because this is exactly how I built my career. Never allow your vision at work to morph into myopia (a lack of imagination, foresight, or intellectual insight), resulting in a "that's not my job!" attitude. Become the *go to person*. Just a word of caution, you will still need to deliver on your day-to-day obligations while you solution for extra credit. Maintaining one's balance is key in achieving success.

If you've never seen the musical, **How to Succeed in Business without Really Trying**, make it a priority to do so. It's hysterical. This show will teach you how to go from the *mailroom* to being *President* in just a few days. Yes, it can take that long...so be patient.

How many Yodelayheehoos does it take to change a light bulb? It's as easy as one, two, three. One, the light bulb will have been changed. Two, everyone will assume it was the Yodelayheehoo. Three, no one will ever really know who did it. "It is amazing what you can accomplish if you don't care who gets the credit." - Harry S. Truman.

****

The "Delegator": Mark Twain said, "Never put off until tomorrow what you can do the day after tomorrow…and put onto someone else's plate". I added the second line. Unfortunately, it's amazing how many who fit this personality type are seen as exceptional Managers; especially when they haven't done a damn thing. What can you do if your boss is a "slacker" who piles all their work onto your plate? Not a hell of a lot outside of bringing it to their attention. If that doesn't work, you may have to bring it to the attention of someone higher up. Slackers make a lot of promises; the majority of which they never keep; e.g. getting you that raise, that promotion. Be prepared to fight your own "battles" to get the recognition you deserve. If you placate and resign yourself to doing their work, you *will* make yourself miserable. Don't do it!

How do you know for sure if your boss is a Delegator? Should he/she use any of the following phrases, there's a pretty good chance they are one: "*Okie dokie; Hunky dory*; *Atta boy*; *Giddy up*; *A-ok*; *Now we're cooking with gas*; *Peachy keen"*; and last, but not least, "*Up to snuff*".

Good Managers and Leaders need to delegate. It comes with the territory. No one person can do it alone. The distinction is, good Managers and Leaders do not pile work, which is their responsibility, onto others, but assign work to each resource based on each resource's responsibility to the job. For example, I regularly need to report to executive management the overall status on multiple programs for which I am accountable for. Each program could have as many as six to ten individual work-streams. The day-to-day activities to manage each workstream fall to Project Managers who report to me, with each Project Manager managing as many as four or five initiatives.

Each week, a collective view of each program needs to be created. I do not ask any of my Project Managers to work on the collective view which includes rolled-up budgets, schedules, inter-dependencies, risks, etc. That is my responsibility. I do make each PM responsible to provide their individual budgets, schedules, etc. which are necessary for me to create the collective view. Week to week, it's not uncommon for me to assign additional work to be performed by my Project Managers; I need the numbers formatted differently; a new matrix; a new Gantt chart, etc. While I certainly have the capability to do these tasks myself (I could have taken what each Project Manager provided in the past and reworked everything myself), designating this work to those who report to me is an appropriate delegation.

If one feels they are unnecessarily being "piled on" with inappropriate requests from a "slacker", immediately start to record and track each and every request made of you. If you are to get anywhere with the "slacker" or upper management in correcting this situation, you'll have to substantiate your position with facts (as if you needed any more work…sorry about that).

How many Delegators does it take to change a light bulb? This one is easy. The number is always equal to the number of direct reports a Delegator has.

****

The "Royal Court": If you're out-of-shape, consider signing up for a membership at the nearest health club and begin a workout routine. Make sure the club offers classes that emphasize how to bow, curtsy and genuflect. This personality type is never singular. It comes packaged as the entire upper echelon of a company; a self-anointed "holier-than-thou" attitude rules supreme. The Merriam-Webster Dictionary defines an "Elitist" as: one who holds a belief that certain persons or members of certain classes or groups deserve favored treatment by virtue of their perceived superiority. The optimum word here is "perceived". This should not be mistaken for the "old boys club" more prevalent at many of the financial institutions. The distinction here is: financial companies aren't resistant to evolution; they embrace it.

I have only witnessed the institution of a Royal Court a few times during my career. Royal Court companies have a long history of maintaining an antiquated "status quo" mentality; sometimes going back over a century. Royal Courts are typically companies where the *perceived value* of the *company's name* is their greatest, and sometimes only, asset. You won't find any of today's start-up companies on *this* register of Who's Who. Today's start-up companies are innovators, leading-edge, and progressive. They're not going to let a "this is how we've always done it" mentality stand in their way of becoming successful.

Royal Courts are fertile breeding grounds for idiots. Without exception, every troublesome personality covered in this book can be found taking up residence at a Royal Court. When you attempt to introduce change, their immediate reaction is, *"that's not part of our culture"*. These bozos just don't get it. It's that very attitude which positioned them behind the eight ball regarding technology and best practices. I equate their antiquated, backwards way of thinking with the moss that grows on a castle's walls; serving only to mask the truth.

I have attempted, on several occasions, to help organizations who fall into this category. And, several times, I have been unsuccessful. My attempts were the only times during my entire career where I could not affect a change. I'm not Superman. I do have vulnerabilities. Royal Courts are pure kryptonite; a crystallized, green meteorite sapping the life force from anyone the royals have deemed as mere peasants; hired only to till the fields and harvest the crops; certainly not to think.

During these engagements, I couldn't help but observe that a vast number of employees and consultants were not happy. Silent were the jubilant voices amongst the rank and file singing, "Hi Ho, Hi Ho, it's off to work we go". Perhaps this accounts for why Royal Courts have an above-average percentage of turnovers among the serfs, a trend that will likely continue until the oligarchy is replaced with parliamentary rule. As Royal Courts continue to lose market share and post poor earnings reports, there will come a time when they will rue the day.

In wrapping up this phenomenon, I can only offer up the following advice: If someone believes they are a "blue blood" and destined to wear the crown; then, by all means, please venture forth on your trusty steed to your coronation. Just watch out for the moat! If not, pack up your few, meager belongings in a knapsack and travel forth to a distant place where the sun smiles upon the land and its people. The grass can be greener, trust me.

How many Royal Courts does it take to change a light bulb? "Hear Ye, Hear Ye. To those both far and near, from this day forth, let it be known throughout the kingdom that only the few who reside in the castle shall glory from the benevolence of divine light."

The "Weasel": Can you picture the horrific scene from the movie, **Alien**, where the infected astronaut is lying on the table in the ship's infirmary; writhing in pain and eventually convulsing as the creature explodes from his chest cavity? Well, there you have it..."pop goes the weasel". Remember, in space, no one can hear you scream!

Do you ever get the sense that something is nibbling away at the foundation you built; the base upon which you built your career? The "Weasel" is a very cunning creature. Known as an active predator, they prey on the unsuspecting. The problem is that it's hard to distinguish Weasels from an ordinary co-worker. By burrowing, Weasels keep their destructive nature below the surface. Usually, it isn't until after the damage has been done that those targeted had any idea that they were prey to begin with.

Why would one person purposely set in motion a plan for another person's destruction? This personality type is one hundred percent convinced that they are *brilliant*; that they know better than anyone else how things should be done, and that *they* should be the one in charge. Weasels never openly reveal their conniving ways. To throw you off their scent, their demeanor will be just a little too cooperative, too agreeing.

The tell-tale signs are subtle. It takes a keen eye. Does someone say "yes" to everything and then never follows your instructions? Does someone always ask for *special considerations* that no one else would ever request? Does someone periodically initiate talks with senior management behind closed doors? Does someone misdirect and cover-up when asked to provide the root cause of an issue they were involved in? And, don't ignore or dismiss it when others bring to your attention the Weasel's small acts of treason. Unfortunately, many do and find excuses for such behavior, e.g. "Oh, he was only trying to do what he thought was right". Unaddressed, such allowances could signal the "beginning of the end".

Should you identify a Weasel in your ranks; let them know you are on to them. Under no circumstance should you allow even one additional minute for the "Weasel" to commit another act of subterfuge. You must immediately implement damage control. Conduct an investigation and find out what was being said behind your back. Reverse the direction of scrutiny from you to them. If you have the authority to have them removed from your team, do so. If not, bring the responsible party who manages the "Weasel" up-to-speed and ask that they find an alternate resource. Why do I suggest removal and not reconciliation? Reconciliation will not be possible. Think about it. Would you ever be able to trust this person again? Highly doubtful!

If it is not possible to remove or dismiss a Weasel, then you need to implement Plan B, having them remove themselves. This requires a thorough fumigation to exterminate the pest.

A mixture of:

One-part: Excessive, in-their-face, micro-management. This ingredient is extremely effective and enters a Weasel's nervous system almost immediately.

One-part: Publicly calling the Weasel out when they do not perform as instructed. Caution: this ingredient has been known to cause the shakes and fits of rage in lab rats.

One-part: Injecting (on the record) official "unsatisfactory" reports (when warranted). Highly effective since there is no known antidote to counter this procedure.

One-part: Any other "uncomfortable act" one can impose to make the Weasel absolutely miserable on the job. Caution: use only prescribed *legal* doses of this ingredient or else one could be sued for malpractice.

Weasels do not like to be challenged, controlled, or made to look inferior. Applying the right amount of pesticides usually has excellent results with the Weasel moving on to less toxic hunting grounds. Should the first application of pesticide not have rid you of the pest, keep applying until you've attained the desired results. Remember to always wear protective gear and apply generously.

How many Weasels does it take to change a light bulb? Who said it needed changing? Did anyone check with the Weasel first? The bulb will be changed when the Weasel damn well says it needs to be changed.

Postscript on Personalities: While I've joked about the many personality types you may or may not encounter on the job, there is a serious side to consider. Please be aware of those who may need your help. Be cognizant of any signs that indicate someone is in trouble; severe depression, suicidal, or manic behavior, etc. Early intervention can help to prevent those in need from harming themselves or others.

Be respectful of each other.

We are us…and us…is all we've got.

Chapter Four – "Who Will Buy"

Who will buy this wonderful morning? Such a sky you never did see.

Salesmanship will serve you well in life. If you've never held such a position, try it. Take a part-time job at an appliance store, a phone soliciting company, or a car dealership. You'll learn about yourself and others...fast. When I was seventeen, a friend and I were driving over to his house one Saturday afternoon and happened to pass a house that had a car on the front lawn with a "For Sale" sign. The sign also stated, "$300 as is". My friend had me pull over, got out, and yelled back for me to wait. I watched as he rang the doorbell and entered the house.

A moment later, he came out, took the "For Sale" sign from the car and threw it in the back seat. He then hopped into the car and waved for me to follow him. When we got to his house, I asked him why he needed another car when he already had one. He said he didn't. I replied, "If you don't need another car, why did you just spend three hundred dollars?" He smiled and said, "I didn't. I only paid one fifty". My friend went into the garage and got two lawn chairs and some sodas. He then parked the car on the front lawn and placed the "For Sale" sign back on the car's windshield. Taking up our positions in the lawn chairs, we enjoyed the afternoon sun and drank our sodas.

Within an hour, a car stopped and the owner got out. My friend met him coming up the lawn. After a little haggling, my friend sold the car at the original three hundred dollar asking price. A one hundred percent profit in less than an hour. I learned that day that my friend's "gift of gab" could talk you out of your last dollar...twice! There are two types of sales people; those who believe in the value of what they sell and those who are only in it for the money. Guess who I would have an issue with?

Over the years, used car and life insurance salesmen have been portrayed as being the "most despicable." This stereotype doesn't always hold water. One of my closest friends owns a used car dealership. He's one of the most honest and straight-up guys you'll ever meet. If you buy a car from him and decide that you're not happy, even a month later, he'll take it back and refund your money. Because of his reputation for honesty, he has a great "repeat" customer base and gets referrals upon referrals. If only everyone could be trusted to do the same, "What a wonderful world it would be".

Do you know how life insurance was invented? One day, a guy walked up to another guy and said, "Hey, I've got a great idea! You give me your money while you're alive and I'll give it back to you when you're dead". The amazing thing is, the other guy said, "Where do I sign?"

I was walking through the mall during the Christmas season when I passed a music store that sold pianos and organs. There was a Help Wanted sign prominently displayed at the front entrance. Since I was still going to college and could always use some extra cash, I walked into the store, found the Manager, and introduced myself. The Manager asked only one question, "Can you play Jingle Bells"? I answered, "Yes". He replied, "Good, you're hired. Go to the front of the store and play Jingle Bells on the keyboard closest to the cash register".

The keyboard was the newest model, the XK-5000, which featured auto-accompaniment. It had more buttons, faders, and knobs than the cockpit of a commercial airliner. Anyone with a little practice and two fingers could sound as if the New York Philharmonic was playing along with them. Within a few minutes, I was playing Jingles Bells with a full brass section playing riffs and drums rump-rump-rumpling along.

About five minutes into my performance, an elderly couple stopped in front of the store to listen. As we smiled at each other, they approached and said how much they enjoyed my playing. I asked them if they were doing their Christmas shopping; the drums were still rat-a-tat-tatting in the background. The couple responded that they came to the mall to buy a new color television set. The set at home was on the fritz and, since they watched their grand-children quite often, having a television was a necessity with little ones.

Suddenly, out of nowhere, the Manger descended like a vulture upon his unsuspecting prey. Taking over the keyboard, he began to explain the awesome features of the XK-5000. I could swear I heard him tell them how it not only played music, but that it could clean the house and cook dinner all at the same time. How? It was the XK-5000 for crying out loud, that's how! Then, the Manager went on to tell them more students got into Harvard and Princeton who played the piano. I was stunned. The sales pitch continued for another ten minutes about the hours and hours of enjoyment an instrument would bring into their house. Mind you, a house without a television set?

As you may have guessed, the couple used their television money to purchase the XK-5000. I was flabbergasted. After the Manager wrote up the sale, he told me to take my dinner break and to be back in thirty minutes. Well, it's been thirty-nine years since I left for dinner; I haven't gone back yet.

Another adventure into the world of sales occurred when I started up a company. I had an idea for a computer-based marketing service, one that afforded companies the opportunity to get in front of targeted customers thirty to sixty days before their competition could. It took several years developing the system and, now that it was finished, I was anxious to begin signing up companies. Being a start-up, I didn't have the cash-flow to recruit and pay for a salesperson. It was going to have to be me. For anyone who has started a business, you know better than anyone that in the beginning you wear all the hats...president, computer tech, accountant, janitor and salesperson ...whatever it takes.

The first account I called on was one of the three long-distance carriers in the U.S.A. I met with the Senior Vice President of Marketing. I explained my company's computerized marketing service and the extraordinary value it could provide. I was also very open that my company was a start-up and needed to attract companies of their stature to participate in order to grow. For their participation, I would offer exclusivity and a discounted rate card for the first two years.

This arrogant, son-of-a-b#tch looked at me across from his desk and said, "We don't need you. We could do this ourselves. We're the biggest and the best". Politely, I countered, "Why would you want to go through all that time and expense to duplicate what I've already accomplished? The same money you would spend to compete would buy your company years of exclusivity and, with the added benefit that the return on the investment could begin immediately since I was already up-and-running". Turns out, this guy was just a ball-buster, an "Intimidator" who probably never came up with an original idea in his life and liked shooting down the "little guy".

Never daunted, I called and arranged a meeting with the second long-distance carrier. When I entered the conference room, much to my surprise, present was not only the Senior Vice President of Marketing, but so was the CEO, CFO, and other prominent members of the company. It turned out that the SVP liked my pitch over the phone so much; he felt it warranted others to be at the presentation. My presentation was identical to my prior presentation at the first company. The story was the story, no embellishments.

A week later, I received a call from the CEO himself. The CEO went on to say, "We were very impressed with your company. We definitively feel we will be able to increase our market share by participating...but what impressed us even more than your service was your honesty. Count us in!" My open, honest, and sincere sales approach led to me signing up many prominent companies. Lies are too hard to remember. The truth never is.

As a kid, I don't think I ever thought about honesty beyond the story of George Washington and the cherry tree. That changed one summer when I was on vacation with my parents. We stayed at a Hilton Hotel. Next to the Bible in the bedside drawer was the biography of Conrad Hilton. I began to read. This was a remarkable man. Hilton never used contracts. A handshake sealed the deal. Hilton made it widely known that his word was his word and he expected the same of those on the other end of the handshake. Hilton also made everyone aware that if he caught you in a lie or, if you had deceived him in anyway, the deal was off, regardless of any benefit he may have derived. The relationship would be over, and he would never do business with you again!

Conrad Hilton's reputation for honesty allowed people to trust the man at his word; something very rare today. This man's story had an impact on me. I have always conducted myself in a similar manner and always will. Not everyone wants honesty. As unbelievable as it may sound, some people actually want things sugarcoated. With me, you're going to get the good, the bad, and the ugly. The same should be said of you.

Remember the executive who told me his company could do this themselves? Bullsh#t! I must have heard that more than a dozen times with each of my start-up companies. No one ever did. Whenever you meet up with one these belligerent jackasses, do yourself a favor; don't become argumentative. Be the better person. Present why your offer is the best possible "bang for their buck", but do it professionally, wrap up and thank them for their time. While not an easy thing to do (most of us would certainly like to tell them off), taking the high road can have its rewards.

On one occasion, as I was leaving an executive's office, his secretary smiled at me and whispered, "Sorry, he treats everyone that way...he's just a bast#rd". A few months later, I received a call from this very same secretary informing me that the "bast#rd" had been fired and that her new boss was much more receptive to opportunities like mine (she'd heard my pitch). With her help, we arranged a meeting with the new VP of Marketing, resulting in another sale. If I had been a jackass on my initial visit by telling the first VP off, that outburst would have been the secretary's impression of me. I doubt that she would have ever made the call.

There are those nights when I come home from work mumbling. My wife instantly knows the cause and will say, "Biting your tongue all day?" Yes, even as outspoken as I am, now and then you must show restraint. Otherwise, you will gain a reputation as a "hot head". Having such a label will not serve you well.

Over the years, I've employed a few techniques to help regain composure when something or someone has *set me off.* If the event was triggered via an email, I immediately write a response. A scathing response! But I don't send it. I keep it in my draft folder. This serves two purposes: One, it affords me some time to calm down and reassess the situation. Often, after a few hours, and I've had a chance to reread my response, I just delete it. Other times, I edit/modify and send it on. The second reason to wait before reacting is; many times, other recipients who were on the original email will have responded, either defusing the situation or have taken on the battle themselves.

If the situation comes about during a meeting, hallway exchange, or phone call, again, I don't respond immediately if other people are party to the verbal exchange. When I get back to my desk, I compose an email response and place it in my draft folder and follow the same procedure previously described. You need to judge each situation as they happen and respond appropriately. Some moments call for putting someone in their place then-and-there. Other times, restraint is called for. Just think twice before you react.

As much as I would like to conduct myself as Conrad Hilton did with only a handshake, such an approach is not possible in today's age of deception. There once was a time (not that long ago), that if you asked a child what they wanted to be when they grew up, the answer would be a fireman, a policeman, a lawyer, and so forth. The answer was a profession; a means to an end. Today, the same question brings back a response of, "rich"; with no regard on how to achieve it. There are many unscrupulous people out there.

The companies I've founded over the years have always had legal counsel; from producing a Non-Disclosure Agreement up to a Prospectus and its subsequent filing with the SEC (Security Exchange Commission). In addition, proprietary and intellectual property rights are always secured (Patents, Copyrights, Trademarks, Service Marks, Trade Secrets, etc.). The same is true when it comes to your company's finances. Have the best representation you can afford. Many of the larger accounting companies have special rates for start-ups and entrepreneurs.

A few last insights regarding salesmanship: creativity is essential for success. I remember telling my father how difficult it was to get local merchants to sign up for my new computerized marketing service. While national sales were going well, sales to the smaller, mom-and-pop retailers were almost nonexistent. I told him how the moment I opened the door to their establishments, they would hold up their hand and say, "Not interested. Go away". It was as if the word **SALESMAN** in bold, capital letters was stamped across my forehead. A week later, I received an envelope in the mail from my Dad. Inside the envelope was a cartoon cut out from a newspaper; nothing else...no letter, no note...just the cartoon.

The cartoon showed a King standing at the top of his castle surrounded by his Knights. The King is looking out onto the valley below. The valley is filled with tens-of-thousands of the opposing force approaching the castle. The head Knight, tapping the King on the shoulder, says, "Sire, there is someone here to see you!" The King, still looking straight ahead toward the valley, responds, "Not now, I'm fighting a war". Standing behind the

Knight is a salesman dressed in a business suit. In one hand, he holds a briefcase which has the lettering: *Acme Gatling Gun Company*. In his other hand, he holds the formidable weapon. The message was simple. The solution to winning the war was there for the taking. The only thing the King needed to do was to take a moment to turn around. He didn't.

The next day, I went on my sales calls with copies of the cartoon. Now, when I entered a store and the merchant held up their hand, I'd walk up without saying a word and hand them the cartoon. A moment later, the merchant would laugh and say, "What are you selling?" The ice was broken. From that day on, the local merchant market became a source of additional revenue for my company. *Dad was always looking out for me.*

The strange thing is I had done something very similar when I was young and first began submitting my plays to publishers. But it never dawned on me to use this technique when selling B2B (business-to-business) as in the previous story. After submitting several of my plays to several publishers, it was quite evident that their responses to my submissions were the standard, run-of-the-mill, form rejection letters. Even the signature at the bottom was stamped.

One day while reading the comic section, there was a Charlie Brown cartoon featuring Snoopy. This was the period when Snoopy considered himself an author and, week-after-week, would be at the typewriter while perched on top of his doghouse. This particular strip showed Snoopy reading a letter (I paraphrase): "Dear Writer: This was the worst story we have ever read. Never before have we received such drivel. We implore you, please, under no circumstances, ever submit another story to us ever again. With warmest regards, The Publisher". Snoopy then looks up and says, "Probably a form rejection letter".

On my next submission, I enclosed a copy of the cartoon. While the play didn't get published, I did receive a very nice response back from the publisher who enjoyed the cartoon, found my including it inventive and ended his letter with, "You can rest assured; this is *not* a form rejection letter. Sincerely, The Publisher".

Finally, do yourself a favor. When you successfully land a sale, shut your mouth. Do not, under any circumstances, continue to sell. There is many a novice who did not follow this simple rule and then talked the customer out of signing the contract. Too often, the "after conversation" is unguarded; resulting in unintentional consequences. Instead, get their signature, thank them, and get out.

Doors can be opened and opportunities can present themselves if you find creative ways to get around, over, and through the many barriers which will rear their ugly heads. Not just in sales, but in life.

One last little piece of advice for those who may consider starting a business. Whenever I have my business cards printed, I have two sets made; one with *President* under my name, the other set showing *Account Representative*. Then, depending on who I am meeting with, the appropriate card is provided. If the meeting warrants an executive-to-executive exchange, guess who I am? On the other hand, I would never go out on a sales call as the President of my company. Why? Think about it. You come to my business establishment to sell me whatever product or service your company offers. You introduce yourself to me as the *President* of your corporation. Trust me, I am going to ask you for every conceivable concession I can dream of. Why not? After all, you're the "man in charge", the "grand poobah", the "king of the hill". Aren't you? Not a good position to be in when it comes to sales. It's always best to leave yourself some wiggle room.

Representing yourself as an Account Representative has many advantages. Now, when concessions are asked for, you can simply inform the other party that you'll take it "under advisement" with your management and get back to them. I did this many times, especially with my software development company. Seemed everyone wanted one more *bell and whistle* than the current software version provided. This approached afforded me time to consider the request and perform a comparative analysis (cost versus benefit).

If incorporating the request as part of my application would increase its overall value and entice other potential customers to "sign on the dotted line", I would modify the code accordingly. On the other hand, if the request was so esoteric that it would only benefit that one particular customer, the request was denied and the application would be offered "as is". It will never be possible to satisfy every request. Weigh the importance of each and every suggestion. Then, act in the best interest of your company and your company's "bottom line".

Chapter Five - "Getting To Know You"

Getting to know you, getting to know all about you.

Interviewing should be fun. You probably think I'm off my rocker. I said it *should be*, not that it *is* for many people. I have always enjoyed the interview process; the challenge of being selected as *the one* to resolve the problem. There are probably hundreds of books written on the subject of interviewing. To be honest with you, I haven't read any of them and, at this stage in my life, most-likely, never will. That doesn't mean you shouldn't if you think they can help. Rather, what I am going to share with you are a few of my real-world, hands-on experiences. To help better illustrate my perspective, I'm going to intermingle both sides of the process; being an interviewee as well as being an interviewer. If you're going to have fun on an interview, two things are necessary; you need to have the right attitude, and you need to be prepared.

I have interviewed and been interviewed countless times; it comes with the territory of being a consultant for over thirty-two years. Consulting gigs can range from three months (an assignment) to three years (an engagement). There is no doubt in my mind, after all these countless interviews, that the average interviewer is not qualified to perform this task. On the flip-side, a large percentage of candidates interviewing are not qualified for the position, either. Talk about a recipe for disaster...a non-qualified interviewer interviewing a non-qualified interviewee. Utterly amazing! Welcome to Corporate America.

At one particular company I was consulting for, I had a team of approximately thirty-six members. Two-thirds of my team members were provided by other departments; not members I had either interviewed or hand-selected. Within the first few months, I had to dismiss several members, as they were not qualified for the positions they held and could not deliver. Almost every resource in these very *necessary* dismissals had been fulfilled by one particular department; one particular Manager. Let's not mince words here...the people I had to let go were from "deep space".

Whenever one of them would be in the vicinity of my office, I swear I could hear the robot from **Lost in Space** warning me, "Danger, Will Robinson". After the second time that a particular position wasn't filled appropriately, I went and visited the hiring Manager. I made a suggestion to improve his interviewing skills. I told him that when he was escorting a candidate to the interview and they were coming up in the elevator together, to ask one simple question, "What planet are you from?" Then I told him, "If the answer isn't Earth, hit the down button, immediately!" I don't think my suggestion sunk in. In fact, I'm sure it didn't, because the next person he placed on my team introduced himself to my Senior Coordinator with, "Take me to your Leader".

On this particular engagement, I had to dismiss more people than any other time during my career (more on letting people go later in this chapter). To correct the situation, I personally took on the interviewing responsibilities myself and, within a reasonable period of time, provided the team with competent resources. Convincing others that you should take on their responsibility takes finesse and negotiating skills; a topic we'll cover in greater detail in another chapter.

Years back, during the heyday of computer consulting, some fly-by-night placement agencies would send just about anybody, as long as they were breathing, on an interview. Eventually, this tactic made it more difficult for the legitimate agencies to distinguish themselves. To help a friend of mine who owned an agency, I wrote a print ad which helped to set them apart. The ad featured a picture of a hot air balloon with a hole at the top, air escaping and plummeting toward earth. The large caption above the picture read: "Houston, we have a problem!" The smaller caption below the picture read: "His resume looked like he could launch the Space Shuttle all by himself. The problem was, he was full of hot air". The ad went on to explain how this agency extensively screened their candidates and only presented an exact match that met their client's needs. Business improved for my friend, and I was glad to have helped.

You, the Interviewee...

Okay, let's get down to brass tacks. You want a promotion or a new (and improved) job? Well, you're going to have to convince someone that *you're* the man or woman for the job, *the best of the best of the best* (as appropriately phased by "J" in **Men in Black**). As I stated earlier, there is a very good chance that your interviewer will be ill-equipped to make that assessment. You're going to have to do some of the heavy lifting here. Be prepared for the same old, worn-out questions like: What would you say is your greatest strength? Tell me one thing that you feel you could improve on?

Could the interviewer be any lazier? There are countless ways to ascertain such information from a candidate without asking those questions directly; ways that would provide real insight, not the stock, prepared bullsh#t answers. So, now that you know this garbage is coming (if you didn't already), make sure your greatest strength answer fulfills the "number one" specific need that this position/job requires (whatever that might be).

The one thing you can improve...that's easy...more education. If a college degree wasn't a requirement, you are pursuing either a BA or BS degree. If you have a BA/BS, you're pursuing your MBA. If you have your MBA, your PhD. Under no circumstances ever reveal anything about yourself that truly needs improving, e.g. "I have a tendency to think I'm Gibbs from NCIS and slap the backside of people's heads from time-to-time. I need to stop doing that."

It is critical that your resume accurately reflects your skills and accomplishments. If you've embellished and get caught in a lie or misrepresentation, you've committed the cardinal sin of interviewing. A qualified interviewer (they do exist now and then) will discover these discrepancies. You will be found out...end of interview...next candidate! However, you do want to talk-up your experiences and capabilities which qualify you for the position. Prior to the interview, you were provided a detailed description of the job's requirements. That was your roadmap. Your homework assignment was to match up as many of those requirements to your experiences in your resume which correlated.

As I stated before, you have to be proactive and point out the similarities and bring them to the interviewer's attention. Now, it may not be possible to have a complete match. More and more companies are posting job descriptions with a "wish list" of skills and experiences that not even Einstein could live up to. If you've been looking for a position, I'm sure you've seen a few like this. Don't be deterred. Usually, the most important and necessary requirements are listed first and go in descending order. If you can match the top five requirements, you are a possible candidate. Go for it!

I'd like to share a few more thoughts on being prepared. Arrive at least fifteen minutes prior to your scheduled time. Never be late. Make sure you have several copies of your resume (please run spell check prior to printing them out), a pad and pen (one that won't run out of ink), and eyeglasses (readily available if you need them for reading). Sounds logical, doesn't it? You don't know how many people I've interviewed who didn't take these things into consideration before entering my office. Have a firm handshake, no wet spaghetti, please! Smile! I repeat, smile! This isn't the Inquisition, it's an interview. If asked if you would like a cup of coffee or glass of water, politely say, "No, thank you". This is a job interview, not a social. Sit when asked to, not before. When seated, sit up, don't slouch. Be engaged. At all times, look the interviewer in the eyes, don't gaze about the room. Listen to each question being asked and answer *that* question and *that* question only. Then stop. Don't babble on. Speak loud enough for the person across the desk to hear you (again, this happens all the time). Never interrupt! I repeat, never interrupt!

Take notes during the interview. And please, not extensive notes (you're not writing a novel), but enough to demonstrate that you are conscientious and professional. Have a prepared list of questions to ask the interviewer when appropriately asked to do so. This is very important. This shows that you have an interest in the position. Make the questions relevant to the company and the job. Again, please don't asks questions such as how many holidays does the company give time off for? Believe it or not, I've been asked those absurd questions more than once. This will work against you. After all, you haven't even been offered the position and your only concern during the interview is about time off? And last but not least, personal hygiene. You need to look like a million bucks...shoes shined...hair combed...clothes pressed, etc. If you look disheveled, your workmanship probably matches. You will never land the job.

The interviewing process is a two-way street. You should be scrutinizing the perspective company as diligently as they are scrutinizing you. When you first arrive at the company, look around; scope out the building and the people in the lobby, including the receptionist. Do they seem professional? Listen in on conversations without being apparent. Do you get an immediate sense that the environment is either hospitable or formidable? Which one did you pick up on? Were you kept waiting to be greeted? When walking with your escort to the place where the interview will be conducted, notice the surroundings. Do people look like they are enjoying themselves? Is the workplace as quiet as a tomb with seemingly no activity?

Is the person conducting the interview your senior or a young, whippersnapper? Are you being interviewed by the person who would also manage you? Can you assess if you have more or less skills and experience than the interviewer? Does the interviewer talk more about him/herself and their great accomplishments than determining yours? Are they hurried? Are they coherent? The reason all these questions are important is to help you in making the decision whether or not you would want to accept the position, if offered. You are not obligated. The decision always remains with you.

I have repeatedly, during my career, turned down offers because I didn't feel comfortable. I often tell my friends that I can find a big mess to cleanup with grumpy people anywhere. I choose not to. I have actually wrapped up and concluded interviews right in the middle of the process. While a rare occurrence, it typically happens when I come to the conclusion that I am talking to a bunch of elitists...or better known as total jackasses. There are a handful of Fortune 500 companies I will never help for that very reason, regardless of the consulting rate being offered.

I had been the senior network/system engineer on a very complex system developed by a major bank and later sold to another major bank for a substantial profit. What I didn't know about the sale came as a complete surprise. I was traded to the other bank, along with the system. I was informed that my new position would start in two weeks.

SCENE: I was told to go to the other bank and meet the Manager I would be reporting to the following day. I swear, the very first words out of this idiot's mouth when I entered his office were:

MANAGER: I hate consultants.

ME: Then, we're not going to have a problem here.

MANAGER: Why's that?

ME: Consider me walking out the door my resignation! *(I proceeded to walk out.)*

When I got back to the bank, as you might have imagined, I was immediately admonished for my actions. I politely informed the "powers-that-be", that I make the decision who I will work with, not them. I did offer to stay on for two weeks and transition my work to other engineers. They accepted.

A few last suggestions: take the time to visit the prospective company's web site. Learn all you can. Is the company publicly traded? If so, review their annual report. Here's a simple question: do you know anyone who is currently, or has in the recent past, worked there? If not, someone who knows someone? First-hand information straight from the horse's mouth can be a mixed bag of truth and fiction and not always one hundred percent reliable. Take anything you're told with a grain of salt. Do an online search via "Google" or "Bing" on the company to glean any other additional information that can help your decision. Glassdoor.com is a web site providing information from various sources, including employees, on many companies.

Lastly, use caution when accepting a position. After all, your goal is to be happy, as well as establish some longevity on the job. If your resume reflects hopping from job to job to job with little duration at each company, that's a big *red flag*; usually an indication that you *can't fit in* or that you *can't do the job*. Not a very good starting point when interviewing; if you're fortunate enough to land an interview in the first place.

You, the Interviewer...

Let's cover the responsibilities of the person on the other side of the desk, the interviewer. If you have this responsibility, please take it seriously. People's livelihoods are at stake. I have actually known hiring Managers who got more of a kick from rejecting people than from doing their due diligence in finding the right person. I am not trying to be pedantic, I just happen to feel very strongly about this subject. Being able to offer a job to someone is one of the noblest things anyone can do. And not being able to extend an offer to someone who interviewed poorly is not the material for jokes around the proverbial water cooler. Interviewing can be a highly stressful situation for many people, similar to the fear many hold for public speaking. Be conscientious, courteous, and prepared.

More than fifty percent of the time when I've gone on an interview, it is immediately apparent that the interviewer has not taken the time, prior to my arrival, to review my resume. This fact, alone, demonstrates how inept many interviewers are at performing this task. It is your responsibility, as the interviewer, to do your homework. Review the resume in advance, and in detail. Mark-up or highlight those sections that pertain to the position's required skills and experience. Have the candidate focus on those areas during the interview so that you can assess their level of competency. Have your list of questions for the candidate developed in advance. Too many times, interviewers "wing it". That is just pure laziness!

Conducting an interview...

Get the candidate to open up about themselves. While you can't ask direct questions such as, are you married, do you have children, etc., you can derive these answers through conversation (or look to see if they're wearing a wedding band). Ask what the commute was like coming to the interview. If the candidate had to take three trains, two subways, and a helicopter, there could be a potential problem. Look very carefully at the duration of the candidate's tenure at their previous jobs. Has the length been indicated in years or in months? Ask specifically why the candidate moved on from one job to another.

How does the candidate handle confrontation? A technique I often use is to state a fact (pertaining to a specific skill in their resume) in absolute contradiction to what the right answer is, e.g. if the answer is white, I say it's black. Then, I gauge their response. What I am looking for is to see how a person might handle such situations on the job. If they cave in and agree, that's a problem.

Are they frustrated and argumentative, or do they stand up and present a compelling case to win me over? How a candidate handles this particular situation affords an insight to an interviewee's underlining personality; something not otherwise easily attained.

I also do something similar when I am on the other side of the desk and being interviewed by an executive of the company. I need to gauge if the company requiring my services can handle being told "No"; if they are an adult, if they are receptive to *not always having things their way*.

At one interview, I was asked if I had previously performed a very specific task. My answer was that, while I had performed similar tasks, I had not performed that particular one. The executive stated, in no uncertain terms, that they need someone who had "done this before". I countered with, "No, you don't. Didn't you just tell me that you recently dismissed a resource with that specific skill that wasted six months of time and a quarter-of-a-million dollars of budget? What you need to recover from the situation is leadership, management, and a driver. I don't know construction either, but if you needed to have this building disassembled and moved across the street, I guarantee that under my leadership it would be done on schedule, under budget, and better constructed than the original building with no additional cost". I started a week later. I also resolved their problem.

If very specific skills need to be qualified and you are not capable of making that assessment, then send them off (if they've passed your initial scrutiny) on to someone who can. If the position requires that the person being offered the job must present in front of others regularly, then set up a second interview to gauge whether they are capable of presenting or not. At one company, we had candidates who passed the initial screening come back and do a PowerPoint presentation to five or six Managers. The one stipulation was the presentation was not to be specific to the job. The candidate could present on how to bake a cake, hang gliding, or whatever. It didn't matter. What mattered was how they demonstrated their presentation skills and addressed questions from the audience.

The ability to present in front of an audience can make a marked difference in one's career. If someone lacks such skills, the theater can be an excellent confidence builder. Theater also provides instruction on team building and management and fosters commitment and dedication. And, participation in the theater isn't only for actors to learn these valuable skills. There is a myriad of opportunities: director, stage manager, stage-hand, prop master, set designer, lighting, sound, wardrobe, etc. If your position requires speaking in front of others and you lack the confidence to do so, get involved with a local theater group.

Stage fright can be overcome. I remember being told that if I got scared on stage to picture the audience sitting in their underwear. This was a supposedly sure-fire way to overcome stage fright. Personally, I always found that image more disturbing than looking out onto a sea of faces.

As an interviewer, your ultimate responsibility is to identify and onboard resources that cannot only perform the requirements of the job, but can, just as importantly, fit in with the team and the organization. After all, do you want to be the one responsible for hiring and subjecting others to a new "Barbarian" or a "Dribs 'n Drabber"? The goal is to reduce the number of caustic personalities in the work environment, not to allow them to proliferate.

Personality and Attitude...

Lastly, a sense of humor is key. I often interject humorous comments during interviews; regardless of which side of the desk I'm sitting on. If an interviewer or candidate doesn't laugh, I have a concern. And yes, what I said *was* funny. This brings us back to the person being interviewed...attitude! At the beginning of this chapter, I stated that if interviewing was going to be fun, it required being prepared and having the right attitude. What is work? According to the Merriam-Webster Dictionary, it is the labor, task, or duty that is one's accustomed means of livelihood. Can you find anywhere in the definition of the word "work" that one should not have fun doing it? Neither can I. Attitude rules, optimism is contagious. It is up to you to present an aura of complete confidence; there is no challenge you can't take on and successfully deliver. Many interviewers are looking for *personality*. I do. Demonstrate that yours would be a welcome addition.

Who wants to deal with someone with a long puss on their face all the time? The next time you go to the office restroom, take a good look at yourself in the mirror. Is yours the face that invites others to engage or run away? If someone is that miserable, they need to do a deep assessment of themselves. Is it the workplace that caused such misery, or life outside the office? If someone needs professional help, they should seek it. I have great respect for psychiatry and the benefits it provides; damn what might be perceived by some as the stigmatism of seeing a mental health professional. Your health, whether physical or mental, is paramount. Never, I repeat, never, let what others might think of you influence the way *you think* and taking action to seek professional help.

About six years ago, I came down with a serious sinus infection. So serious, that it started to affect my mental state. The condition lasted for months. I was having difficulty swallowing which resulted in an eating disorder. Although I was seeing a "specialist" (an Ears, Nose, and Throat doctor), I was misdiagnosed. The infection was mold-based, not viral, and the medications I had been prescribed exacerbated the situation. I continued to lose weight and became depressed. Part of the problem stemmed from a choking incident I faced twenty-five years earlier. This incident resulted in an eating disorder.

Rather than seeking professional help at that time, I faced the challenge alone. It took years to fully recover and be able to eat many of the foods I had enjoyed prior to the choking incident; especially a good filet mignon. My present condition connected me back to my prior affliction, worsening the situation. The only difference this time was, I went to see a mental health professional. I refused to be a victim again and suffer for years while attempting to "heal thyself". I also went to see a General Practitioner who I had been going to for over twenty years. The moment she walked into the examining room, she knew immediately that whatever treatment was being administered by the *so called* "specialist" was not working, so she took charge! She sent me for a battery of tests and to see a new "specialist" (one *she* was confident in), and had communications with my mental health professional.

In a relatively short period of time, the sinus infection was under control, my mental state and eating disorder were vastly improved, and I was becoming my old self again. As I write this, six years later, I just thought you should know that I'll be going out tonight for dinner at one of the best steakhouses in Hoboken, New Jersey.

It is everyone's responsibility to make the workplace congenial. After all, we are all going to spend the largest portion of our waking hours "on the job". The personalities depicted in this book will certainly do everything possible to impede that directive, making it that much more imperative that you do your part to contribute to and foster a congenial environment.

Let me show you to the door...

Unfortunately, some people aren't going to make the grade. Letting someone go is never easy, even if the person has been an idiot or total jackass. Everyone has bills to pay. Some have a family to support. Finding a new position isn't a walk in the park, especially today with the economy being what it is and jobs being scarce. This is why I always present every opportunity for someone whose performance is sub-standard, to turn things around and save themselves. You can't do it for them; you can only afford the opportunity.

Whenever I am faced with such a situation, I immediately have a one-on-one with the person. I need to understand why they are not performing. Are they in over their heads or maybe going through a personal crisis? Only then can you provide the proper guidance. I had inherited one Project Manager who consistently failed to meet his deliverables. After a frank discussion, it came down to being nothing more than laziness. This Project Manager had some good qualities, as well. If not, I would have dismissed them right then and there. There was more than enough time during their weekly schedule to get down to "brass tacks", roll up their sleeves, and do the nitty-gritty. There are aspects to every job that are unpleasant: writing status reports, reconciling budgets, reviewing action items, and chasing down those who are delinquent isn't fun, but it's necessary.

Unfortunately, when one procrastinates day after day, week after week, it becomes almost impossible to catch-up. I offered this Project Manager my help to get caught up and get back to square one. I also put a plan together to help him maintain being compliant going forward. In my Senior Coordinator's office, I listed, on a white board, his reoccurring daily, weekly, and monthly deliverables; when they should start and their respective due dates.

After several weeks of work to get him back on track, I saw

him leaving for the day, walking right past my Coordinator's office. One of the things we had agreed upon was that, at the end of each day, he was to go to the white board and check off the completion of that day's deliverables. This was to be backed-up by sending me proof. I came out of my office and asked where he was going? He told me he was "calling it a day"; that he was tired. I reminded him of his obligation to update the white board per our agreement. He marched into my Coordinator's office, picked up a marker, and proceeded to place check marks next to several deliverables. I asked him what that meant. He replied that it meant all deliverables for the day were done.

Again, I reminded him that, per our agreement, he was to provide proof that the day's deliverables had been accomplished; and that I hadn't received any such materials today. Nonchalantly, he said that he forgot and that he would log on when he got home and send them to me. Funny, I look young for my age, but I don't think I look like I was born yesterday. So, I informed him that proof was required prior to his departure. Otherwise, I could only conclude that the work had not been finished.

He immediately became indignant, supporting my suspicions, and reiterated that he was tired and was not going to go back to his desk, boot-up, and provide what I asked for. I instructed him to do as I asked and that if he didn't, there was no reason for him to return tomorrow. He immediately pulled his company laptop from his bag, placed it on my Coordinator's desk (who had been sitting there throughout the whole episode), removed his badge, and threw it on the laptop; all the while informing me that he didn't have to take this sh#t. I asked my Coordinator to call Security and inform them that I would be escorting so-and-so out of the building and that, under no circumstances, was he to be let back in.

Just as I had suspected, after he left the building, he called the executive I was working with about my dismissing him. That got him absolutely nowhere. However, the next day, the executive asked if it wouldn't have been better if I had found a replacement before dismissing him so that a proper transition could have been done? Smiling, I replied, "Transition what, stupidity?"

You might be thinking, why tell *this story*? Why didn't I tell some funny story about somebody I had to dismiss (and I do have a few)? But, even in those situations, the humor is "dark". As I stated before, letting someone go is hard. I feel for people; even those deserving of being fired. However, once you make the decision to let someone go, never revert.

I've had people actually start to cry and give me every excuse you can imagine as to why their performance was sub-standard. Do not cave in to this display of emotion. If you handled the situation correctly from the beginning, you've already provided several opportunities for them to improve and turn the situation around. If it's reached this point, then, obviously, they didn't apply themselves when they had the opportunity to do so.

I related this story because it serves two purposes: One, if you are in a position of leadership, ultimately, the work-effort of those who report to you, is your work-effort. There is no escaping this. Helping the Project Manager to get back on track was required, whether it ended with him being retained or let go. In addition, it would be very unrealistic to hand over a mess to a "new" hire. Two, since I've always picked up the workload of anyone I've dismissed until I can find a replacement, I need to have an "in-the-weeds" perspective to keep things moving and on-target. Too often, I've seen so-called "Leaders" simply drop the ball when one of their team members didn't work out for one reason or another, allowing those initiatives to flounder and sink into utter failure.

The best way to avoid having a situation which might result in a dismissal is to avoid it materializing in the first place. When I make a final selection of a candidate for an open position, the final conversation with the candidate is a very open and frank discussion on what the position entails and their responsibilities to the job and to the team. I lay out both the good and the bad and that this is their opportunity to "bail" should they believe they possess neither the capability nor desire to meet my expectations. You'd be surprised how many hiring Managers don't spell out what they expect from their prospective candidates. I always do. My teams have fun tackling the challenges we've committed to. But, it's still work and some days won't be a walk in the park. Those days can be brutal and can test everyone's endurance right up to the breaking point. My teams meet their objectives. So, if someone is looking for that "cushy" job where they won't have to tax their brains and produce time after time, make sure my name isn't in any way associated to the posted position.

I had an amazing English Professor for my English Honors and

Theater Art courses in college, Ms. Rita Licciardolo. I'll never forget the first day I met her. I and about forty other students were sitting in a classroom waiting on her arrival to begin the first class for English Honors. As I watched the door, a short, stout woman walked in, stood at the front of the room, and perused the faces looking back. If she had been wearing military fatigues, I could have sworn I was looking at my drill instructor from the Army. This was not meant to infer that there was a physical resemblance, it was *pure presence*.

I immediately got the sense that this was a "no nonsense" woman. I was right. For the next fifteen minutes, she informed the class that this course was going to be remembered as the most grueling ordeal when they looked back on their collective college memory. Dozens of papers were to be researched, written, and submitted. Dozens of books were to be read, analyzed, and discussed. As I looked about the room, I saw the shell-shocked faces of students asking themselves, 'What did I sign up for?' I think there were even a few with a tear or two running down their cheeks. As quickly as it began, it ended. We were ceremonially "dismissed" as she marched from the classroom.

On Thursday, when I entered the classroom, I couldn't help but notice a distinct change from Tuesday's class. There were only six of us in total. Rita entered a moment later. She looked about the room as a big smile formed on her face. "There, now that's more like it", she said! Rita brought her chair from around her desk and sat. She then motioned for the six of us who were scattered about the room to come join her "down front".

Rita explained that the overcrowding we witnessed in Tuesday's class happened every Fall. Students, she explained, have a tendency to think English is easy and that an opportunity to get four credits instead of three, since it was an honors course, made it even more attractive. Rita saw it quite differently. This course was for students for whom English was essential to their purpose. Tuesday's "doom and gloom" speech always saw to it that the "riff raff" was eliminated; like separating the wheat from the chaff. She reminded us that, while the course wasn't going to be quite as horrific as she initially portrayed, it wasn't going to be a piece of cake, either. It wasn't.

I was always quick to recognize a life lesson whenever one presented itself. This was one of those times. I learned that a few dedicated individuals will always *win out* over an army of the *non-committed*; that team building requires setting the stage to find "the few". I tucked this lesson away for future reference when I would have a need to find "the few".

Chapter Six - "Just the Way You Are"

I took the good times, I'll take the bad times, I'll take you just the way you are.

One of my favorite quotes pertaining to perception is: "In the Kingdom of the blind, the one-eyed man is King". How you perceive the world and others, and how the world and others perceive you, are entirely different; of this I'm certain. Very few people are completely honest with themselves. Many become their perceived selves and live their lives as such. Introspection is a difficult task. After all, it's not easy for many people to admit to themselves their faults; that they might be lazy, a liar, dishonest, etc.

At the same time, more and more people are posting their antics on Facebook, Twitter, YouTube, and the like, affording others an opportunity to form their perceptions based on these snippets of bad behavior. In the words of Aldous Huxley, "There are things known and there are things unknown, and in between are the doors of perception".

One day when I was parked outside the Blue Cross/Blue Shield building on Washington Street in Newark, New Jersey, I had the rare opportunity to see "mass" perception in practice. It was a beautiful, Fall day. I was outside leaning up against my car waiting to pick someone up. Suddenly, the crowd of people on the sidewalk started to move hurriedly, parting like the Red Sea.

Lumbering up the sidewalk was the largest man I had ever seen. He stood approximately six-feet, ten-inches tall and weighed in the vicinity of two-hundred-and-eighty pounds. His clothes were dirty and ragged, and he was caped from his neck to his boots in a stain-covered, black slicker. His hair was wild, unkempt and went down past his shoulders. His beard was as full and unkempt as his hair and had grown halfway down his chest. He was a very formidable presence in comparison to the many men and women dressed in their business attire. Emanating from his mouth were constant grunts and incoherent speech. It was no wonder people were running scared. I was to later learn that this was almost a daily occurrence and that the large figure was commonly known on the street as "Mountain Man". The label was very appropriate.

Being the noon hour, parked along the street, lunch trucks were lined up serving business people from the many surrounding corporate buildings. I watched as "Mountain Man" made his way to one particular vendor. As he reached the serving window, he held out his hand and made a series of grunts. Within seconds, an arm extended from the truck producing a hotdog. "Mountain Man" quickly grabbed it, took a large bite, and then looked in my direction.

Now, having spotted me leaning up against my car, "Mountain Man" slowly made his way toward me, step-by-step. I continued to look him directly in his eyes as he approached. When he got within a foot of me, he stopped, leaned forward, and said softly, in perfect English, "Would you like a bite?" He then winked, turned, and walked away in character, grunts and all. It was classic! Who was fooling who?

Age can definitely influence perception. A few years back, I was driving home on a country road after visiting a friend who lived in Pennsylvania. There were two cars in front of me and two cars behind me, all a safe distance from each other and traveling at 45-miles per hour. Coming in the opposite direction was a large, pick-up truck.

Out of nowhere, a seven-point buck ran toward the road from the opposite side. The buck, attempting to jump the pick-up truck, caught his two front hoofs on the top of the cab; sending him into a summersault, nine or ten feet into the air. I watched, in what seemed like slow motion, as the buck descended, back-first, toward my windshield. I closed my eyes and prepared for the impact.

Glass shattered everywhere. My face, hair, and clothing were covered, and even the inside of my sneakers had shards of glass in them. To this day, I still don't know how I managed to pull my car over to the side of the road without crashing into anything (my eyes were still closed). Fortunately, the buck bounced off after hitting the windshield and didn't continue through to crush me to death.

Having witnessed the event, the two cars behind me pulled over to the side of the road. Getting out of the first car was an elderly gentleman who asked with concern, "Are you alright?" Exiting the second car was a young kid who said with great enthusiasm, "That was spectacular!" Age and perception, what else can I say? Amazingly, there wasn't a single dent or scratch to my car. Only the windshield needed to be replaced. I suffered a minor concussion from the impact but, besides that, was unscathed.

Human nature has not altered in two hundred thousand years. When compared to the age of the Earth, which is 4.54 billion years, we humans haven't been around for all that long. While we may be better housed, clothed and fed, and have technology, we haven't evolved very much in terms of our basic instincts and emotions, i.e. love, hate, jealousy, envy, wants, needs, fears, anger, anxiety, laughter, tears, hunger, thirst, curiosity, sympathy, and on. I don't doubt for a minute that a few cavemen were idiots and interacted with their fellow cavemen much the same as present day idiots do.

SCENE: To prove my point, a famous anthropologist discovered cave paintings dating back over sixty thousand years ago. They translated as follows:

GROG: Thak, ooko boki (Fred, get in here.) *Thak enters Grog's cave.* Thak, sro gruel Wooly Mammoth baa urk. (Fred, I want you to put together a presentation that shows the advantage of a Wooly Mammoth having a stick at each end.)

THAK: Gro ut jarti....? (Are there any particu...?)

You get the point. How has your evolution progressed?

While perceptions can mislead, they can also provide valuable lessons if one is willing to be open and honest with him/herself when proven wrong. Preconditioning has a direct effect on one's perception. I was in my last week of basic training while in the Army when I had a severe pain on my right side. The Drill Sergeant had me go on sick call the next morning. The doctor discovered that I had a hernia and immediately sent me to the Post Hospital. The following morning, I was in surgery. A week later, I was back with my unit and was placed on "light duty" for thirty days while I recuperated.

SCENE: One of my assignments was to walk to Battalion Headquarters to drop off and pickup paperwork for Company B. The first day I walked to headquarters, I was faced with an enormous building. There must have been over two dozen ways to enter the huge complex. Somewhat perplexed, I stood there for a moment or two and then made my decision and entered. I had been doing this same routine for a week when, on this particular morning, a General was standing in front of the building. As I approached, I immediately saluted:

ME: Good morning, sir.

GENERAL: Excuse me, soldier. *(I stopped, turned and faced the General at attention)* You know, soldier, I've been watching you for a week.

ME: *(Surprised.)* You have, sir?

GENERAL: Yes. And, I noticed that every morning you choose to enter headquarters the same way. And, I was wondering why?

ME: Well, sir…you see, that door says private…and I'm a Private.

Yes, you read it right. I had been using the General's private entrance for a week. Fortunately, the General had a sense of humor and showed me which door I *should* have been using. I'm positive that this incident was *the story* at the Office's Club that evening. Now, in my own defense, it wasn't entirely my fault. As I mentioned earlier, preconditioning can affect one's perception. Back at Company B, Buck Privates (no stripes yet), were relegated to using certain facilities, specific walkways, entrances, prescribed times to eat, taking a smoke break, and on and on. Now, when faced with a decision (as simple as choosing an entrance into headquarters), the eight weeks of prior regimented conditioning had me on auto pilot. Believe me, I learned my lesson and, from that day forward, I have always given some thought to any preconceived notions I may have before rendering a decision.

A good example of people who don't practice this lesson is what I've coined the "Parental No". When asked a question which can enlist either a "Yes" or "No" response, the parent's instinctive response is, "No". Picture a child asking Mom if they could go over to Johnny's house to play. Mom instinctively says, "No!"

Why? Well, it certainly isn't the hour; it's two in the afternoon. Is it because tomorrow is a school day and homework still needs to be done? No, it's Saturday. Is the family going somewhere later that same day? No. Are relatives on their way to the house for a visit? No. There wasn't a reason. It was a reaction.

Many times, people, not just parents, bring the "Parental No" to the workplace. They react before they think. They didn't really listen to what was being asked. If they had, they might have asked some intelligent questions as our fictitious Mom should have: "Where's Johnny live again?" "How are you getting over there?" "Do his parents know you're coming over?" "You have to be back home by 6:00 p.m. for dinner, remember?" On the flip side, had there been a legitimate reason for not approving the request, it should have been explained, not just an authoritative, "No!"

At work, you are not someone's parent (although some people act like children); you are not their authority, either. You are a co-worker, even if you own one hundred percent of the company. Here's my *Listener's Guide for Good, Better, and Best*: If you've always listened twice as much as you've spoken, you're *good*. If you're someone who hardly lets someone else get a word in edge-wise, listening four times more than you speak would be *better*. And finally, idiots should keep their mouth shut throughout the entire conversation…that would be *best* for everyone. That'll never happen.

Another "faux pas" people often commit during a conversation is formulating what they are going to say next, rather than listening to what the other person is saying. When I was younger, I had this bad habit myself. I would often find myself making mistakes by not following the instructions given to me during a conversation. The reason? I didn't have a clue what the other person said. There I'd be, nodding my head in agreement throughout the entire conversation, all the while, concentrating on what I was going to say next. Have you found yourself doing this from time-to-time? If so, there's help. It's not going to be easy. It'll take a concerted effort to concentrate on what the other person is saying and dismiss your own thoughts as they pop into your head. Similar to a musician attaining Carnegie Hall status…it takes practice, practice, practice. You will be the better for it. And, by the way, *never* pass up an opportunity to ship your kid off to one of their friend's houses!

We make the majority of our most important decisions in life based on a lifetime of conditioning and perceptions, thus one's ability to *accurately* perceive and comprehend is crucial. If one is truly up to the challenge and completely immerses him/herself, such an understanding can lead to self-actualization; a feat most people will never achieve. Why? With such realization also comes the knowledge that one can never go back. One can never plead ignorance. Hence, the saying, "Ignorance is bliss", will never again apply. For many, *not* knowing is a happier state of being than knowing.

Letting go of one's preconceived "self" is not easy. And should you let go, there *will* be trials and tribulations to endure; no ifs, ands, or buts. There are a slew of books on the subject of attaining self-actualization. But, two of my favorite pieces of fiction which help to illustrate the journey are by the author, Richard Bach; **Jonathan Livingston Seagull** and **Illusions, the Adventures of a Reluctant Messiah**. In **Illusions**, which takes place in present day time, the protagonist, Richard, is having difficulty understanding how the Messiah's abilities are in all of us; that what the Messiah has attained, anyone can achieve. To help Richard, the Messiah tells the following story (I've paraphrased):

In a land there lived a colony of creatures that clung to the rocks at the bottom of a river. Day in and day out, all that the creatures did was to cling. For this was their way of life. One day, one of the younger creatures asked the elders if there was anything else to life beyond clinging. The elders responded, "No. This is all there is to life". The younger creature replied, "But there must be more? I'm bored. I think I'll let go". The elders became indignant, "Are you insane? If you let go, the river's current will smash you against the rocks and you'll be dead quicker than boredom". To which the younger creature said, "If this is all there is to life, I'd rather die than cling to this rock any longer". And with that, he let go.

As fate would have it, the elders were proved right. The river's current was strong and swift, and smashed the younger creature against the rocks, one after the other. The pain was almost unbearable. 'Perhaps', he thought to himself, 'I should have listened. I don't know if I can go on'. But something inside him would not allow himself to give in, to give up. Through his suffering, he began to understand; to achieve an awareness of his existence, far from of a life of clinging. Now near death, the river's current slowly began to lift him above the rocky bottom. Soon, he was riding the current near the surface of the river; beyond pain, beyond fear.

Time passed. Then, one day, he floated over a colony of creatures like himself clinging to their rocks. One of the creatures looked up and saw him and said, "Look, a creature like us, yet he flies. Truly, he must be the Messiah". The younger creature yelled down, "No, I am a creature like you. All I did was let go", as the river's current took him further and further away until he was out of sight and only a memory. But the creatures of the colony below did not understand. And so, they continued to cling. For this was their way of life.

Woody Allen tells a story where he's kicked out of his college metaphysics class for cheating on the exam. The professor caught him peering into the soul of the girl sitting next to him. The approach I'm about to reveal might just provide you with the ability to do the same. So, keep it to yourself. While in college, for my English Honors course, the final paper was a thesis. My dissertation put forth a theory that one could exercise the five senses (and beyond if one was so inclined; e.g. intuition, pre-cognition, etc.) through a form of sensory meditation. It was simple in theory, difficult in practice.

Here's an encapsulated version for those who may wish to put theory into practice (you didn't know when you purchased this book there was going to be a homework assignment). The premise is to start with a small, uniformed object; such as a solid marble. For five minutes, one would use their senses to discover everything conceivable with regards to the object: sight (color, hue, imper-fections, dimensions, shape, etc.); taste (if applicable); hearing (tapping, rolling, bouncing, etc.), smell (if applicable), touch (texture, hardness, etc.). Later that same day, one would re-engage the object and again go through a discovery process for an additional five minutes. During the reengagement, new discoveries are always revealed.

Slowly, over time, one would increase the complexity of the object and the duration of discovery until, ultimately, the goal would be to sit in a room (the object) for hours (the duration) for both sessions. Your ability to perceive will be heightened far greater than the average person could ever achieve without the benefit of meditation. You will become acutely aware of your physical surroundings. An added benefit will be your perception of people - their mood, body language, facial expressions, posture, voice inflection, behavior, etc. - providing you a distinct advantage in your day-to-day interactions.

The level of commitment and discipline to implement and reach a state of "heightened awareness" is not something easily achieved. To be quite honest, while I have shared my thesis with many friends over the years, I am not aware of anyone else who has undertaken the challenge. Perhaps you will? "The world is full of magical things, patiently waiting for our senses to grow sharper." - W.B. Yeats

Some people's ability to perceive can be extraordinary. I'm taken back to the day a patient arrived on the mental health unit who claimed he was from another planet. I know for a fact that this was his first visit to the unit, as I had been working at the facility since the day it opened. The patient entered the unit walking backwards. Not once did his head move to the right or left; not even slightly. It was amazing how he navigated the unit, never bumping into a person, a piece of furniture, or a wall. When asked for the first time to go to a specific location, i.e. the dining area, Community Center or the Nursing Station, he never asked for directions. Somehow, he knew instinctively where to go; at a brisk, backwards pace.

Whenever I would engage him in conversation, I would have to remind him that he was on planet Earth and not speak in his native, planetary language. He would reply, "Oh well, if I must. Your language is *so primitive*". When I asked him the reason for his visit to Earth, he answered, "It will all be revealed on the last day of the Mayan calendar". I had no idea what he was referencing. I didn't know a Mayan from a Cayenne. Over time, with the help of the doctors and staff, plus a few medications, the patient came back down to Earth. I don't know if that was a good thing or a bad thing. I and others found him fascinating as he was. Maybe he *was* just a visitor to a small planet. We'll never really know (cue the spooky music).

Fortunately, his predication based on the Mayan calendar

didn't come true. I did take the time to go to the library and research his reference to the Mayan calendar. While the majority of you had only been aware of the approaching "end-of-time" prediction for a year or two, I had been watching the clock count down for over four decades.

On December 22, 2012, I was sent the following cartoon in an email showing two Mayans. One guy is down on the ground working on a stone tablet. The other is standing next to him and asks if he'd like to go and have a beer. The guy chiseling away says, "Sure, why not. It's not like if I don't finish this it'll be the end of the world".

Be careful what you reveal about yourself. Stay off Facebook, Twitter, or any other social media site. If you've already established yourself on any of these sites, close your account immediately. No, I'm not old fashioned. I'm as into technology as anyone; I do it for a living. Social Media sites can provide great benefits as a marketing tool for businesses (as with the promotion of this book), political campaigns, etc., but can have disastrous results for the individual who socializes "a little too much". Don't let your fifteen minutes of fame be for something stupid. Save it for something important that matters. If I have to explain why, there is no hope. And, should you not take my advice, at least keep what you reveal about yourself to a minimum.

Revealing oneself can come in many disguises. One day, the unit Physiologist at the mental health facility suggested that he administer the Rorschach test for the fun of it. For those unfamiliar, this is what is commonly known as the inkblot test; ten cards given in a specific order, one at a time. The recipient looks at the inkblots on the cards and tells what they see; simple, but quite revealing. The doctor held up the first card. After a moment, I told him I saw a man and a woman having sex. He held up the second card. Again, after a moment, I told him I saw a man and two women having sex. He then held up the third card. Immediately, I responded that I saw an entire room filled with men and women having an orgy. The doctor said, "You seem to be preoccupied with sex". I answered, "Me? You're the one holding up the dirty pictures". There was no way I was going to tell the doctor what I really saw in those inkblots. The goal was to remain an employee at the facility, not a guest.

It's nobody's business to know the utmost details of who you are and what makes you tick; especially to others "on the job". One, the majority of people don't give *one iota* about your personal life and two, those who "seem to care" will, most-likely, make trouble for you. Keep it to yourself.

My eventual "moving on" from my position at the mental health facility wasn't due to money or a disinterest in my work. It came about unexpectedly by means of an extraordinary life-changing event which occurred one afternoon. Whenever something was missing from the kitchen; the salt and pepper shakers, ketchup, mustard, etc...there was only one place to go looking. Robert's room. Robert was an elderly gentleman who was a classic hoarder. Anything and everything that wasn't "nailed down" on the unit eventually found its way to his room. On this particular afternoon, the lack of salt and pepper on the tables in the kitchen resulted in my paying Robert a visit.

Robert was sitting on the edge of his bed when I entered his room. He seemed more despondent than usual. So, I sat in the chair to talk with him. What occurred next is almost impossible to describe. As we talked, a strange feeling came over me. Not strange in the sense that I felt ill, but strange in an ethereal sense. The room took on an aura of soft light and Robert's voice faded until it was no longer audible. Then, in an instant, I witnessed and felt everything that had transpired throughout Robert's entire lifetime, all the pain and suffering. It almost knocked me out of the chair I was sitting in.

When I came walking out of Robert's room, I must have looked visibly shaken because the unit Psychiatrist immediately asked me if I was alright? I tried my best to explain to the doctor what just happened. The doctor smiled and said, "You've been given a great gift; one that most people will never experience in their lifetime. You've seen the soul of another human being". It didn't seem like a gift. It disturbed me for days. Perhaps I cared too much. But, I knew that I never wanted to have that experience again. It was too painful. When it came time to renew the contract, I moved on.

Everything in life is relative to one's perceptions. Science has made great strides in understanding the complexity of the universe. Yet, our understanding of the "God Particle" is in its infancy, and may never be revealed. Today, Einstein's theories are being challenged. But, in understanding the presuppositions behind

Einstein's special theory of General Relativity, much is still relative today (no pun intended) and challenges my grey matter almost daily (all I have to do is look up into the night sky). Even his simple explanation of space and time, written for those of us not educated in the science of "mathematical apparatus of theoretical physics", boggles the mind.

Suppose you came to see me off at the train station (by the way that was very nice of you). As the train leaves the station, you are standing on the platform waving goodbye. I am on the train hanging out the window waving back. As the train builds up a "head of steam" and starts to travel faster, I drop a stone I found in my shoe. From my vantage point on the moving train, the stone travels in a straight line to the ground. But, from your vantage point on the stationary platform, the stone travels in a parabolic curve on its way to the ground. How can the stone appear to have traversed on two different trajectories by two separate observers?

Answer: Each observer's relative "position" (the train and the platform) relative to each observer's "time and space". If you'd like to have some fun, pick up a copy of Einstein's book.

For many, the moment perception becomes thought...then thought becomes reality. But it's an illusion. For my play, **Two for the Price of One** - a psychological thriller – the challenge was presenting cues as both fact and fiction to lead and deceive; to alter the audience's perception at various stages of the play; slowly layering suspense until the final moment when the murderer is revealed. The play opened with the following scene.

ACT ONE, SCENE ONE: The curtain rises on a dingy, studio apartment located in a high-rise tenement building somewhere in New York City. The furniture is old and worn. You can almost smell the mildew coming across the footlights. The apartment is a far cry from resembling anything even close to being luxurious; making it a perfect match for the surrounding neighborhood. Now and then, traffic and the sounds of sirens can be heard coming through the two wide, open windows against the back wall. Seated in the living area are George and Ellen Myers. Each occupying their own wingback chair; each engaged in their own activity. George is reading the newspaper as Ellen knits. Neither is paying much attention to the soft, big band music coming from the radio situated on the small table between them. It's a hot, humid summer night. We begin to hear voices coming through the open windows from the alley below. While we can't distinguish what is being said, we can tell that the voices are that of a man and a woman arguing. Ellen hears it, too.

ELLEN: *(Stops knitting and looks at George. Her voice is almost a whisper.)* Can you hear that? I think its Alice. It sounds like her. Alice from the apartment down the hall? *(Pointing her finger stage right.)*

GEORGE: *(Paying no attention.)* Umm.

ELLEN: *(Now, in a somewhat louder whisper.)* George, didn't you hear me? I said, I think its Alice. *(Ellen lowers the volume of the radio located on the table between the wingback chairs.)*

GEORGE: *(Still reading the paper.)* So what? *(Slight pause.)* She's a slut.

ELLEN: *(Rising slightly from her chair and leaning toward the windows.)* Somebody's with her. It sounds like a man. *(Ellen now finishes her rise from the chair and begins to walk to the open windows.)*

GEORGE: *(Now, for the first time, pays attention and looks up.)* Get back here! Sit down! *(With disgust.)* Damn it! Get back here!

ELLEN: She sounds like she's in trouble. *(Ellen continues to the windows.)*

GEORGE: I said, get back here! It's none of our damn business what that slut does.

ELLEN: *(Leaning forward and looks down onto the alley below.)* It is Alice! I can see her. *(Leaning out the window a little further.)* I can't see who she's with. *(The voices below steadily get louder as the couple in the alley continues their arguing.)*

GEORGE: *(Now out of his chair, crosses to Ellen and pulls her back from the windows and back to her chair.)* What'd I tell you? Mind you own damn business.

ELLEN: She might be in trouble, George.

From the alley we can hear Alice pleading 'No, please, you're hurting me. Please.' Alice's last sound is a scream,

'Nooooo...Nooooo.' Followed by a gun shot. Ellen races back to the open windows and looks down on to the alley.

ELLEN: George, I can see her. She's not moving. She's just lying there.

GEORGE: *(Again crossing over to Ellen and pulling her back from the windows.)* Damn it! Get away from the window before somebody sees you.

ELLEN: She's been shot. George, we've got to do something? We should call the police. *(Begins to reach for the phone located on the table between the two wingback chairs.)*

GEORGE: *(Grabs Ellen by the wrist, preventing her from picking up the phone.)* So what if she's been shot? What's that matter to us? We're not getting involved.

ELLEN: *(Almost in tears.)* George, please. We should help. She's just lying there.

GEORGE: I said no! We're not gettin' mixed up with the police. Anyway, it's one less whore walking the streets. Who's gonna miss her?

ELLEN: *(Ellen breaks George's grip and again reaches for the phone.)* I'm calling. *(George tries to stop her but Ellen pulls her arm back.)*

GEORGE: *(Making a fist at her as he walks back to his chair.)* You get away from that phone! We ain't callin' nobody!

ELLEN: Why? Why are you like this? It's Alice, George. She never did anything to you. Why? Because she was pretty and wouldn't give you the time of day. Because you couldn't control her like you control me?

GEORGE: *(Angrily.)* Shut your mouth!

ELLEN: I saw the way you always looked at her.

GEORGE: *(Even Angrier.)* Shut up!

ELLEN: *(Calming down.)* No, George. No more. Not now. I'm calling the police.

GEORGE: (Getting out of his chair.) The hell you are!

ELLEN: *(Very calmly.)* Yes, George. *(Slight pause.)* You know, Alice and I were somewhat alike. Both of us alone and afraid. The only difference, *(another slight pause)* she didn't have the same man to remind her every night.

George, dumb struck, sits down slowly as Ellen picks up the phone and dials.

Fade to black.

Curtain.

Alice's death was the defining moment, the catalyst which provided Ellen the courage to stand up to what we can only perceive as years of abuse from her husband. Perhaps her life will be the better for it. Perhaps not. Why do people stay in bad relationships, bad jobs, bad anything? The fear of the unknown? An apprehension about "letting go"? It's hardly uncommon to find people in situations they'd rather not be in, but remain in. Like the younger creature who finally rid himself from a life of clinging, unless one is willing to accept that there will be some bruising, any hope of a better life can never be attained.

Let go…

Chapter Seven – "You've got to be Taught"

You've got to be taught before it's too late, before you are six, or seven or eight.

Today, political correctness has gone amuck in every aspect of our lives. A day doesn't go by that there isn't at least one story on the evening news that doesn't reveal just how far gone our society is. One day, the news reported on a five year old boy who was expelled from kindergarten for kissing a five year old girl on the cheek. Under that criteria, I would have been expelled weekly. Another day, there was a story about a twelfth-grader whose teacher told her to take off her tee-shirt because it had a picture of a political candidate the teacher was opposed to; and when the girl refused, she was escorted from the building.

Then, there are those organizations that want to stop the Nativity from being displayed at Christmas and people from saying Merry Christmas; school boards stopping Halloween parties and costumes from being worn to school because some kids may not have the money to buy a costume. Are you kidding me? These idiots came to the conclusion that such children are deprived. So, in their infinite wisdom, they deprive them even further. Brilliant! And, I don't want to hear about all that psychological crap they always use to base their decisions on. That's pure bullsh#t. Kids are resilient. Did the school board really think that these same children wouldn't be resourceful enough to improvise some sort of costume and go trick or treating later that night?

Now, the "idiots" have Easter in their sights. It's not an Easter Bunny or an Easter Egg, it's the Spring Bunny and Spring Egg. Their warped way of thinking is, "We need to be tolerant of others who may not share our beliefs". What? Really? How about those who don't share our beliefs being tolerant of us? Especially since our traditions have been around for hundreds, if not, thousands of years; have never hurt anyone, and we never asked or forced anyone to share in those beliefs.

Then, there's the college professor who had students write the name of Jesus on a piece of paper, told them to place it on the ground, and stomp on it. When one student refused, he was expelled from class and brought up on charges of misconduct. People, are you going to condone this idiocy running rampant in our society? Please say, "No", and then mean it by taking action whenever someone or some group's perverse rhetoric attempts to uproot and destroy the good that makes us great.

Never before in my lifetime have I ever met so many wimpy cry-babies as I have with today's younger generation. Perhaps I feel this way because of my upbringing. Our home was warm and loving and fostered creativity and independence. No one got a new car when you turned seventeen. What you got was the family station wagon, which came with conditions, i.e. running errands, driving your sister somewhere, etc. If you didn't want to pitch in, you didn't get the car. Period. You made your bed every morning, mopped and dusted your room. You helped to set and clear off the kitchen table every night. You took out the garbage and performed many other chores. My brother and I also had to mow the lawn, rake leaves, shovel snow, and help Dad, who always had a home improvement project in progress, i.e. a new kitchen, remodeling the bathroom, building an addition, finishing the basement, and on and on.

I know what some of you are thinking. No, we didn't have to walk up hill both ways in a snow storm to go to school. Believe it or not, we had fun. No one complained. We didn't get an allowance, we got a job. At twelve years old, I started a lawn mowing service. My father leant me the money to purchase the mower, and I paid him back from my profits. I mowed sixteen lawns at a buck-fifty per lawn. The summer I turned fifteen, I did aluminum siding installations; a sixty-hour work-week at one dollar per hour. I was the richest kid in the neighborhood. The following year, I got my WSI certification and was a lifeguard for the next two summers.

There were no hand-outs. What we got was self-reliance and a sense of achievement. We were a family, and families work together. My parents also did a very unique thing at Christmas. I've never known any other parents to do this, not back then and not any parent since. On Christmas morning, as you opened your gifts, you had to read the tag before you could rip off the wrapping. Only *one* gift was from Santa. All the other gifts were from Mom and Dad. This was to teach us that there were limitations to what one could ask for. The stack of gifts weren't gratis from Santa; Mom and Dad were responsible for the bounty. I wouldn't trade my childhood with anyone else's in the world. Those memories are priceless and bring a smile to my face often.

Our parents also taught us *right from wrong* and to think before we committed ourselves to an action that could have consequences. They also taught us to use our *common sense* and listen to our innate, inner voice. Everyone has that voice. Some listen, some don't. And then, there were those seemly small but important lessons. I remember my Dad telling my brother, sister, and me that when picking out a Christmas or birthday present for Mom, it was never to be something for the house, like an appliance. The gift needed to be something special and personal, not something that would result in performing a chore around the house. Dad went one step further with my brother and me and said, "One day, you're going to have a girlfriend and eventually a wife. Under no circumstances are you to ever buy a gift that *slices, dices, or makes Julienned fries*. If you make that mistake, I guarantee you'll find yourself in the doghouse".

My wife and I know many parents with children of varying ages, from infants to college students, and a few with young adults who are *finally* out on their own (I added the word finally for their parents sake...but most of these kids are still very dependent upon Mom and Dad). What some kids get away with today is appalling. We have witnessed kids in public telling their parents "No" when they've been asked to do a simple request. We hear parents boasting how their children don't have to do anything around the house, how they take them everywhere, buy them everything, and do everything for them. For the parents who are like this...wise up!

These parents have done their children a huge disservice and have set them up for failure when they enter the "real world". Kids are being taught that *everyone needs to be a winner*. Sorry, everyone doesn't get to be a winner; there are winners and losers; *it's called, Life*. Kids need to be prepared for it; otherwise, they are going to find life very hard and disappointing. Parents aren't *buddies*! Parents are *disciplinarians*!

Every single one of my childhood friends who, to this day,

have a great adult relationship with their parents, had parents who were disciplinarians. I know of other kids from my childhood who walked all over their parents. These parents are now alone in their senior years. Those kids made sure they stayed as far away as possible so that they wouldn't have to take on any personal responsibility. How dare their elderly parents interfere with their having a "good time"? If parents allowed their children to be selfish and self-indulgent when they were kids, what else could they have expected when the kids became adults?

My brother and I both enlisted in the U.S. Army. My brother served from 1967-1970, and I served from 1969-1972. After I graduated high school, my father came up to me one day and said, "Let's go get an ice cream", and proceeded to drop me off at the recruiting station. I'm joking, folks. Actually, my father's talk with me went something like this: you can go to college, but I don't know where we'll get the money; you could get a job, but I don't know what kind of job you'll get without a college education; or you could join the service and have the G.I. Bill help out with school after your service. The choice was obvious. There's a saying about serving in the military; it's a million dollar experience you wouldn't pay a dime for.

But putting the saying aside, it *was* a great experience. You grew up fast. You learned to work as a team. You became someone whom others could depend on to carry your share of the load, and more, when necessary. You faced challenges and met them "head on". There was no retreat. On the day each of us left for boot camp, my brother and I were on our own and took on the personal responsibility for being adults from that day forward.

The most important thing a parent can do is listen. Really listen. Not just going, "ah ha" in the background while a child is opening up and sharing. My Mom was *the Mom* that every kid, boy or girl, came to talk with in the neighborhood. She was a great listener. She never made a judgment on their behavior; good or bad. What she would do was help them to come to the right decision on their own simply by asking questions. It was like watching Perry Mason.

I remember the time my brother had such a conversation with Mom. He had just turned seventeen and was dating a girl a year younger. There was going to be a house party on Friday night he wanted to go to. The problem was the girl's parents had "nixed" any chance of that happening. They didn't want her in cars yet (my brother had just gotten his license) or going to a house downtown where they didn't know the parents. My brother's plan was to have the girl sneak out through her bedroom window, go to the party, and then redeposit her without her parents being "any the wiser". When he finished, he sat there looking very proud of himself for devising such a cunning scheme.

Mom then asked my brother a few questions. "Do you like this girl?" The answer was, yes. "Do you want to keep seeing her after Friday night?" Again, the answer was, yes. "What do you think will happen if her parents find out that she disobeyed them?" My brother said she'd be in a lot of trouble. "Do you think her parents would ever let you see her again?" The answer was, no. "They'd be right in taking that action, wouldn't they? After all, how could they trust you, again?" The answer was, yes.

My mother wrapped up her summation with, "I'm not going to tell you what to do. You do what you want to. Just remember, whatever the outcome, it was your decision". My brother and his girlfriend didn't make the Friday night party. They did see each other the following day, and for many days thereafter. Now, my brother wasn't dumb. He already knew what the right thing to do was before he even had the conversation with our mother. Remember the innate, inner voice? What he needed was a sounding board. He needed reaffirming.

Unlike the time of my childhood, many of today's parents find it very difficult to accept criticism when it comes to their children. Then again, there are those parents who aren't adults themselves (children raising children). While my perspective in prior paragraphs may have sounded harsh, I believe it was necessary. One last thought, consider a famous quote by Albert Einstein: "I fear the day when the technology overlaps with our humanity. The world will only have a generation of idiots". Unfortunately, Einstein's fears have come true.

And, it's only going to get worse. You only have to turn on the television or look at the front-page of a newspaper to confirm that today's kids have been anesthetized, leading to anti-social be-havior. Today's parents must immediately enforce restrictions on a child's use of technology, i.e. cell phones, texting, computer games, etc...if not, the loss of basic communication and social skills can never be recovered later in life.

Parenting is a difficult task.

Please take it seriously.

Thank you!

Chapter Eight – "The Meeting Song"

Don't waste our time with trifles and don't be bureaucratic.

In the next few chapters, we're going to cover some day-to-day business etiquette specific to dress code, meetings, emails, hallway conversations, the Christmas party, maintaining one's office space, and the like. If you didn't know these activities had certain "protocols", you do now. Let's start with a high-level, common sense review of meetings. I'm sure somewhere in America there is a college that offers a degree in Corporate Meeting Protocol, a certified CMP program, as well as dozens of additional "no-hope-of-ever-getting-a-job" majors.

Let's cut to the chase: your participation in a meeting will, more than likely, be one of three roles: the chairperson / facilitator, a presenter, or an attendee. If you are the chairperson / facilitator (in most organizations, both roles are combined into one), your responsibility includes arriving early and having *everything* prepared in advance: conference line established, the projector or video conference capability functioning, presentation materials organized on your laptop to be displayed, etc.

If you are fortunate enough to have a Senior Coordinator (as I have been for the past ten plus years), this person has the responsibility to print "hard copies" of all presentation materials as a "fall back" position. Trust me, projectors, laptops, and other devices do fail from time-to-time.

Prior to the meeting, the Coordinator would have attached and emailed presentation materials to everyone on the invite. If equipment was required (projector, easel, flip-board, etc.), the Coordinator would have pre-arranged it. Should you not have a Coordinator, the previous lists of tasks are your responsibilities.

During the meeting, the Coordinator takes meeting minutes

and captures all action items as directed by the chairperson. If such a role does not exist, the chairperson must assign this responsibility to another participant. Under no circumstances should the chairperson perform this function. The chairperson's job is to see to it that the purpose for having the meeting is successfully accomplished: keep people focused, assign action items, settle disputes, etc. Presenters at the meeting are to have their materials to the Senior Coordinator at least two days in advance of the meeting for their review, inclusion, and distribution.

I am not going to go into every possible reason for having a meeting .i.e. weekly status, brainstorming session, one-offs, and so on. There are countless reasons for having a meeting, the majority of them are bogus and a waste of everyone's time. Meetings are usually a good excuse for not actually performing the work required to get something accomplished. I've consulted for companies that had meetings to plan meetings.

As wasteful as meetings are, they've become part of the corporate landscape. So, how do you get the appropriate *bang for your buck*? Participation, participation, participation. That doesn't mean simply having a bunch of people show up in the hope that food is going to be provided. It means having the *right people* in attendance and the right people being *one hundred percent engaged*.

On my most recent contract, the senior leadership informed me that it was very difficult, in their corporate culture, to get people to attend meetings and, for those who did attend, arrive on time. I looked at my Senior Coordinator and saw the smile on her face. It was obvious what she was thinking after working with me for over ten years, 'these people don't know Doug.' I smiled back.

True to their statement, at my first meeting, only a handful of people showed up, and even those few people arrived late. My Coordinator, as we always did, immediately resent the calendar invite followed by an email with one sentence: *We're waiting!* Simultaneously, I would be out the door hunting people down and personally escorting them to the conference room. Upon seeing me approach, the response would always be the same, "I'm coming, I'm coming. Just wrapping something up".

Once I had everyone assembled, I'd look at the time and state that fifteen minutes had been wasted. I'd inform everyone that by now the meeting typically would be concluding rather than just starting; that I know we're all busy and that we've got a lot on our plates, as I do. I didn't admonish them any further (at this point, they got the hint), rather, I simply said, "Okay, let's get started". It doesn't take long for people to realize that my meetings aren't like the majority that they attend.

One, they are fun (we have a lot of laughs – more on humor in another chapter); two, they are focused (no going off topic). Three, they are short (cover what needs to be covered, wrap up, and get on with the business at hand). It usually takes once, at most twice, with this approach to get attendees to cooperate. From that point forward, you never delay starting your meeting on time waiting for stragglers. After a few weeks of conditioning, it's amusing to see "the expression" of those who made it on time give to those who arrive late.

Having a productive meeting requires that all participants are one hundred percent focused and engaged. I do not allow attendees to accept cell phone calls, text messages, or work on their laptops during my meetings. Instant Messaging is a big "no-no", as well. I've actually witnessed people with six, seven, or more IM windows all going simultaneously. What made this even more ridiculous was that these idiots were messaging with other participants in the same room. Supposedly, this would allow them to exchange information that couldn't be shared "out loud". Seriously? The majority of these IM messages were "put downs" and "inside jokes" on other participants in the conference room. So juvenile!

I also do not establish a conference line unless it is absolutely necessary for participants who, for *very legitimate reasons*, can't attend in person. Even in these cases, I only socialize the dial-in number with those specific participants. I want to look participants in the eyes! I want to see that they are paying attention!

Back a few years ago, I facilitated a meeting in which a senior engineer dialed into my meeting (although he sat in a building less than a quarter-of-a-mile away – which happened to be, mind you, the same building where my office was located). After he announced himself, I asked why he wasn't with us in the conference room, as well as the whereabouts of two other engineers who reported to him and were requested to be at the meeting. All three engineers' input was critical to several agenda topics to be covered. He responded that he was very busy and felt he could better manage his time by joining the meeting by phone. He also informed me that he didn't know the whereabouts of the other two engineers.

I politely told him, "bullsh#t", and that I was driving down to the other building to pick-up him and the other two engineers. I was no sooner in my car when my Coordinator called on my cell phone to tell me that the senior engineer couldn't locate his missing engineers. I asked her to relay the message that I would *now* be coming into the building. The word spread quickly that I was on the prowl. The senior engineer met me as I reached their section of cubes. The two missing engineers were poking their heads up-and-down from their cubes like gophers. If I had a big mallet, I swear I would have played "whac-a-mole".

Without me saying a word, one-by-one, they all gathered around me. I escorted them to my car and then to the meeting. Back in the conference room, I apologized to the waiting participants for the delay and began the meeting. From that day forward, regardless of what building an invitee was in, everyone knew better than to not attend my meetings in-person, not arrive on-time, and not be engaged.

You might be thinking, 'What a hard ass! Cut me some slack!' I don't go to the job to make friends (although I make many). I go to the job to make people productive...while earning their respect. Yes, there is always some resentment at first. Why won't there be? When I first arrive on many of my engagements, it is immediately apparent why they have a track record of failure. No one has held them accountable. Now there is someone who does. But, I do it in a positive way. I don't purposely embarrass, berate, or belittle. I will repeat this next line many times throughout this book, respect is earned and earned daily. You never cash in on past laurels (to rely on one's past achievements and cease to strive for further successes).

You might be surprised to learn how quickly the right leadership comes to be appreciated, especially as success replaces failure. Success is addictive. The majority of people in the workforce want to succeed but find it difficult due to a number of idiots standing in their way, constantly erecting barriers. Prior to the right leadership taking corrective action, many see themselves as mice trapped in a maze, constantly running into *roadblocks*, *dead-ends*, and *endless circles*. When someone finally comes on the scene who has the expertise to remove these barriers, it is a *welcomed relief*. Within a relatively short period of time, it's not uncommon for me to hear comments like, "We weren't making much headway until you took over the program". I appreciate that people recognize my contributions. Removing barriers is a Leader's *job one* priority.

I have countless examples of removing barriers. But one initiative stands out due to the sheer numbers which were erected. On a Sunday evening, I received a call from a very senior Manager who was accountable for a program whose visibility went to the highest level at the bank, the Chairman of the Board, the program's sponsor. I had known this particular Manager for twenty years and had worked with her several times during my career. Over the years, we had become very good friends. Three months earlier, the bank had contracted one of the "Big Six" consulting firms to head up the program. Although the initiative had kicked-off as intended, the program's schedule and deliverables were now three months behind. Absolutely no progress had been made (while a lot of money had been spent on inflated *partner billing rates,* which is typical with the "Big Six"). It should be noted that the program's overall budget was twenty-six million dollars, nothing to sneeze at.

To make things even more stressed, the Chairman had announced at the annual Shareholder's Meeting earlier in the year that the initiative was going "live" on September 9th. It was now June 9th, leaving only three months to bring the program back from the cliff. If not, it would end in embarrassment for the Chairman. My friend asked if I was available to help out. I said I was.

That evening, the Manager provided several dozen documents (via email) and asked if I could be at the bank Monday morning at 8:00 a.m. I stayed up until two in the morning reading all the documentation and making notes. Shortly after I arrived on Monday morning, the Manager escorted me to a conference room where the team had been assembled. The room was filled with

one unhappy face after another. The Manager then introduced me
and left...closing the door behind her. There was a new sheriff
in town!

The *roadblocks*, *dead-ends*, and *endless circles* the team
faced were numerous. Paramount was the system's hosting
platform. What had been promised by the third-party vendor and
what was delivered were at completely opposite ends of the
spectrum. The vendor's blunder resulted in my implementing an
immediate deep-dive to re-architect everything: from hardware
to infrastructure to code. This was no small feat. This task
alone took weeks to re-engineer and re-cost. The next barrier
brought to my attention was the fact that the development team
was unable to code. Why? They didn't have an environment
to code to! They had been told by the head of building
maintenance that no additional equipment could be placed in the
development lab. Hard to believe, but the developers had been
twiddling their thumbs with absolutely nothing to do for over six
weeks prior to my arrival.

I immediately met with the head of maintenance and
asked, "Why?" He told me that the room was at capacity; that
the lab's room temperature was already too hot and couldn't
handle any more equipment...not one more piece. I thanked
him, left his office, and then visited the lab. What I discovered was almost beyond comprehension. These idiots had
vented the two portable cooling units into the ceiling, recycling
the heat right back into the lab. Unbelievable! Once I instructed
maintenance to install a dual window vent, the problem was
resolved, equipment was installed, and coding could commence.
I should point out that even after I brought the issue to the
attention of maintenance how to rectify the problem, the head of
maintenance didn't want to follow my simple instructions. I
reminded him that the sponsor for the initiative was the Chairman
of the Board and that he either cooperated or I was making a
visit to the Chairman's office. His choice!

The next situation was getting all the Production equipment racked-and-stacked in Brooklyn in preparation for the
"go-live". The Project Manager responsible for installing and
configuring the site informed me that the installation was
underway and would be completed on schedule. I thanked him,
hung up the phone, and then took the next subway down to

Brooklyn. I entered the building and went immediately to the fourth floor to Cage D, Racks 1-26. Empty! All of the program's equipment was still in their original boxes, stacked, and piled on the floor.

I left the building and took the next subway back. I went to the Executive Vice President's office and informed her of the "screw up" in Brooklyn. The EVP immediately picked up the phone and called the President of the company responsible for racking and stacking the equipment. It was not a pleasant phone call. The President was read the *riot act*. The EVP finished up the call stating that everything had better be completed on the date contracted, and she didn't "give a damn" if the union workers had to work around the clock and paid double-time, triple-time, or whatever-time…on the President's dime. We weren't spending a nickel more. The end result…the situation was resolved practically overnight.

These were just a few examples of more than a dozen barriers that were thrown up repeatedly, day after day, hampering the team. Once all the barriers had been removed, the team successfully delivered and went "live" on the day announced by the Chairman, September 9th. Unfortunately, these situations aren't uncommon. In fact, they're prevalent in program and project management. Why weren't these problems addressed by the prior leadership or management? It's not like these barriers were going to miraculously resolve themselves. Most of the problems were known right out of the starting gate.

Unfortunately, a large percentage of those who are *in charge*, for who this responsibility falls to, have a tendency to bury their heads in the sand when barriers surface. This explains why, according to the latest statistics, greater than eighty percent of all programs and projects fail. It takes a very specific personality to take on any and all obstacles and follow through to a final resolution. It takes someone who is willing to get off their butt, roll up their sleeves, and won't take "No" for an answer. There wasn't a day that went by on this initiative where one or more team members didn't thank me for removing barriers which prevented them from doing their jobs successfully.

It should be noted that those who erected barriers had a very rude awakening. On the day I took on this mess, the CIO handed me two "virtual" tools. One was a pair of sneakers and the second was a sledgehammer...with the following instructions: "When someone gets in your way, put on the sneakers and try to run around them. If that doesn't work, take out the sledgehammer and let'em have it!"

And so it is with meetings. Meetings are typically non-productive and better be worth the investment of everyone's time and energy. Meetings need to be focused. How many times have you witnessed a question being asked to someone on the conference line only to hear them ask for the question to be repeated or for more information? Here's your answer...they weren't paying attention. Few people on the phone ever do. If you are the facilitator, it is your responsibility to make meetings productive. If you are incapable of performing that function, then relinquish the responsibility to someone who can. In football parlance, meetings need to move the ball forward (decisions need to be made, action items need to be implemented)...they are not a timeout.

Too often, meeting organizers think quantity over quality is what makes for a "good" meeting. I have actually witnessed, on more than one occasion, the "big top" mini-bus phenomenon. I'm sure you've witnessed it, as well. You and your meeting participants are patiently waiting outside a conference room for the prior meeting to end. Finally, the door opens and person-after-person-after-person-after-person exits. It's inconceivable how they could pack that many clowns into a room.

I was contracted by one of the country's largest telecom corporations to recover a worldwide implementation that was going very badly. My first day on the engagement, the CIO had arranged a meeting to bring me up-to-speed on the situation. When we entered the executive conference room, forty-five people were gathered around the football-field-length table. The meeting lasted for more than two hours. As the CIO and I were walking back to his office, he asked me what I thought of the meeting. My answer was straight forward, as always, "There were forty people too many, and it was an hour-and-a-half too long." The follow-up meeting had five participants meet for thirty minutes.

At another meeting with the same company, the chair-person must have owned stock in the 3M Corporation. They came "loaded for bear" with a dozen different color 3x3 sticky note pads. Fifteen minutes into the meeting, the four whiteboards were covered from top-to-bottom with a rainbow of the little, sticky squares. I was color blinded. While I understood the intent, the method, itself, was a distraction and created confusion. Remember the time-tested mantra: K.I.S.S. Keep it simple, stupid.

Okay...let's *recap*. By the way, this is exactly how a facilitator wraps up *every* meeting. The final moments of the meeting should be a quick review of what was discussed, action item assignments, and next steps. Then, within one day (no longer), meeting minutes, action items, and any follow-up meetings are to be sent to the appropriate recipients.

If you are an attendee, be respectful by showing up on-time and be an active participant, not just a bystander. You were invited for a reason. If you are a presenter, have your materials developed and provided in advance so that edits (if necessary) can be applied and approved. Presenters are to know their materials inside-out and backwards...do not read, word-for-word, what is depicted in your presentation deck. Your deck represents talking-points. Make it interesting. Make it informative. If you are the chairperson, lead by example by doing what you ask of others. Foster cooperation and do whatever is necessary to make sure everyone's participation is worth the investment of their time. It is your responsibility to see to it that everyone has an equal voice at the table; a focused voice, not ranting.

One of the best Webmasters I ever worked with (we'll call him Larry), had only one flaw, he was a complainer of the "first degree". While many of his complaints were legitimate, his going on and on about his problems hijacked the weekly status meeting, frustrating the other team members. The question was how to handle such a dilemma. By no means did I want to silence Larry. At least ten percent of his complaints were in one way or another related to my initiatives. At the same time, I didn't want the weekly meeting confiscated *one hundred percent* by Larry's complaining. The solution was simple. Each week, prior to the status meeting, I would meet Larry at his desk and walk with him to the conference room. By the time we'd reached the doorway, Larry would have gotten everything off his chest, and the meeting stayed focused. Find creative solutions. If you don't care, no one else will. That goes for everything you do in life.

I use my calendar for purposes besides meetings. I have my Coordinator block time across my calendar for repetitive tasks I need to perform; budget reviews, preparing materials for the Executive Steering Committee or Strategic Planning Counsel, etc. My Coordinator also has full privileges to every team member's calendar and forwards invites to critical meetings they are chairing so that they are reflected on my calendar. Why? Simple! In the event that they are unable to chair a meeting (an emergency, sickness, etc.), I can respond accordingly. If my calendar can be adjusted, I can chair the meeting in their absence. If not, my Coordinator can reschedule the meeting to accommodate my calendar. It's all about coordination and communication. Time doesn't stand still while waiting on someone's return to the workplace. It is your responsibility to be able to step in, when necessary.

Our last topic is the agenda. You say you're too busy to put one together and send it out in advance of the meeting? Well, you just shot yourself in the foot. How can anyone expect others to be prepared and to participate if they haven't had an opportunity, in advance, to know what the meeting is about? An agenda does not need to spell out, to the nth degree, the reasons for the meeting. Rather, the agenda should be no more than a list of topics to be discussed, who the point-person is who will lead the discussion for each topic, and its duration in minutes, i.e. <u>SCCM Packaging as a Service, D. Glaeser, 30-minutes</u>. Any supporting documentation should have been attached and sent as part of the original invite. Agendas, if not depicted in the original invite, should be indicated as: <u>To Be Provided</u> and sent at least one day in advance of the meeting.

This is Meeting Protocol 101.

Chapter Nine – "Return To Sender"

**Return to sender, address unknown. No such number.
No such zone.**

Email protocol is critical to one's success in the workplace. Unfortunately, email has just about completely replaced the personal visit and phone conversation as the preferred method to communicate. IM (instant messaging) is yet another unfortunate means of communication in common use. The reasons I state that these means of communication are unfortunate is that these alternatives have replaced *in-person* interaction; and the myriad of benefits which could otherwise be derived: eye-to-eye contact, body language, facial expressions, etc. For those very reasons, still to this day, I get up and go to see people first, if not feasible, call, and as a last resort, send an email.

Emails proliferate like rabbits. We've all seen it countless times; leave two emails in your Inbox, go to a meeting and come back to hundreds all jumping up-and-down, screaming for attention. A properly constructed Subject Line will definitely help to ensure that *your* email grabs your intended reader's attention and helps to elicit a timely response. Below is how I've structured my subject lines which have produced excellent results over the years.

RESPONSE REQUESTED:

Brief Subject Description - Today's Date
Used for the first request, cc: appropriate team members.

2nd REQUEST – PLEASE RESPOND:

Brief Subject Description – Today's Date
Second request, cc: additional appropriate team members
cc: recipient's manager.

3rd REQUEST – PLEASE RESPOND:

Brief Subject Description – Today's Date
Third request, cc: additional appropriate team members, cc: recipient's manager, cc: manager's manager. Note: if a third request does not elicit a response, you need to address this immediately via an in-person visit or phone call (if the person is not local) to determine why there has not been any cooperation after multiple attempts.

CRITICAL:

Brief Subject Description – Today's Date
Used sparingly or else your emails will be seen as the "boy who cried wolf". This subject heading is for truly "critical" instances. Use with discretion. cc: all appropriate people, as deemed necessary.

QUESTION:

Brief Subject Description – Today's Date
Used when you need a quick and simple answer to a non-critical question. cc: all appropriate people, as deemed necessary.

HELP:

Brief Subject Description – Today's Date
Used as an informal, friendly way to enlist someone's assistance. Most people will find it hard to ignore a simple plea for their help. As with the header Critical, to be used sparingly. No cc: Direct communication only.

ANNOUNCEMENT:

Brief Subject Description – Today's Date
Used for just what it states: an announcement, e.g. an upcoming event, personnel changes, etc. cc: all appropriate people, as deemed necessary.

IMMEDIATE ACTION REQUIRED:

Brief Subject Description – Today's Date
Used when the action is time sensitive, but not at the level of being critical. Use with discretion. cc: all appropriate people, as deemed necessary.

PLEASE REVIEW & CONFIRM:

Brief Subject Description - Today's Date
Used when a confirmation in writing is required.   To: line should include all recipients who are required to review and confirm. cc: all appropriate people, as deemed necessary. Note: A Vote button can be set up to enlist and store a Yes / No, or any other type of response.

FOLLOW UP:

Brief Subject Description – Today's Date
Used when following up on emails for Headers: Question, Help, Please Review & Confirm. Subject description and recipients should be the same as the original email.

NOTIFICATION:

Brief Subject Description – Today's Date
Similar to an announcement email, but carries more importance; e.g. pending network outage, interruption of service, etc. cc: all appropriate people, as deemed necessary.

Being organized is a *must* to being successful. It is far too easy to have a slew of email requests fall by the wayside, never to be addressed until they resurface as a problem. The simplest and greatest tool for getting back a response to your emails is the *Follow Up* folder.

The very first thing I do when I start a new engagement is create a Follow Up folder in Outlook. Every time I send an email which requires a response (not all emails do), I drag the *sent email* into my Follow Up folder. In addition, I place emails which require a response back from me, into this folder, as well. Once a day, I review all emails in the folder, starting with the oldest and work backwards. If I received a response back in my Inbox for a particular request, I delete it from the Follow Up folder. If a response had not been forthcoming on an email, and a reason-able period of time had passed (typically anywhere between one and three days - all depends on what was being requested), I resend the request with a brief, "How is this progressing"? I repeat this process over-and-over until I finally get an *appropriate* response (this is where 2nd Request, 3rd Request, etc. come into play).

I emphasized the word *appropriate* for very good reason. Now and then, certain idiots will respond back with just about any bullsh#t they can dream up to get you off their backs. Do not equate an email reply with a response. A reply does not constitute a response unless it adequately satisfies the request. When a reply doesn't, you need to call this out immediately. Do not be polite. Tell them, straight up-front, that they need to cooperate, intelligently (if they are capable).

Instant messaging…what can I say? Some people live by it, others, such as myself, do not. In fact, my IM is never turned on. I am very well aware of what the perceived benefit of this tool is supposed to be (it's in the name – *Instant*), but I find it a distraction, while my Coordinator does not. I am not going to dwell on this. My only word of caution is: please do not become robotic and lose the art of communicating with your voice.

Believe it or not, one day I was copied on the following email from one of my Project Managers: *dan i x belve u got what i ws syng at the mtng yr repl x aswer the qstions i ask so cld u pls aswer the qstions i nd thes 4 a mtng tmr thx*

Was he serious? I called him into my office and asked, "What's up with the new email format?" He told me it was the latest thing in writing; similar to texting. It was a real time saver. Really? A total disregard for capitalization, grammar, spelling, punctuation, and context to save what, two or three seconds? This was the one and only of these emails he ever sent. The format and visual aspects of an email should always be taken into consideration. It makes for readability and clarity. A good tip is to write as you speak. Too many times, in an attempt to make their writing sound important, people use fancy vocabulary. That's what dictionaries and thesauruses were invented for. If you lack writing skills, take an evening course at a local community college; Basic English 101.

As a Senior Management Consultant overseeing many pro-grams, initiatives, and their respective resources, I can be inundated with up to three-hundred emails or more in a day. Hopefully, you don't have this same situation. But, regardless of whether your Inbox receives five emails or five-hundred, you have an obligation to review and respond (if appropriate). I hear the same gripe every day from people: "I can't get caught up on my emails". The funny thing is many of these same people were part of the problem to begin with. They're the ones who never get off their butt and speak to people face-to-face or pick up a phone.

While it's impossible to respond immediately to every email request with an appropriate response, you do need to acknowledge receipt of the request. Nothing is more frustrating than not knowing if your email was even read; that your email, piled on with more recent emails, has worked itself so far down in the recipient's Inbox, to never again surface and be taken into consid-eration. You must take time, periodically, during the day (even if you have to arrive early or stay later) to review each and every email.

I organize my Inbox and my "My Document" folder to be almost identical; segregating each initiative and their sub-categories, and *their* sub-categories in a hierarchal manner. Now, when I review emails, there are three possible actions I can take: if the email has no relevance, it's deleted; if the email required a response, I acknowledge receipt of the request by informing the sender that I am working on it, followed by placing the email into my Follow-Up folder (described earlier); and finally, relevant emails not requiring a response are placed into their respective sub-category folders for future reference. If an email contained an attachment, the documents are placed in their respective sub-category folder under My Documents which correspond to their Inbox equivalence.

Right about now, some of you are thinking, 'This guy's a little anal'. Quite the contrary. The slang "anal" has come to mean equating something with little importance to be equal to something with great importance. Now that email has become the *de facto* means for communication, it needs to be attended to via a professional and organized approach. The greater your communication skills, the better served you will be in business and in life.

Our last topic: The Email Wars (the faint sound of Taps can be heard in the distance). We've all been, at one time or another, a casualty of an email war. Most of the time, these wars are nothing more than a skirmish and extinguish themselves quickly without causing harm; other times, the war is a full scale, global invasion, and takes days before the dust settles. This is a public relations nightmare. Under no circumstances should one ever initiate an email war. Should there be an attempt to recruit your services, do not enlist or allow yourself to be drafted into the fray. This will only show you in a bad light with those in authority. You'll be easy to spot; you'll be the one covered in bandages.

Chapter Ten – "Every Breath You Take"

**Every breath you take, every move you make,
I'll be watching you.**

The hallway conversation is another means to achieve success. If you're like me, you need to get answers, you need to get status, and you need to get results. Since most of us are in too many meetings already, interaction in the hallways, while not ideal, is better than scheduling another meeting. So, how do you handle a one or two minute hallway conversation to get the most out of it? One, you never challenge someone for not getting back to you on a request. Instead, ask if there is anything *you* can do to help them to help you. Two, be respectful of your surroundings. It's a hallway. People may be in cubes, offices, and conference rooms in your immediate vicinity; being loud is disruptive and impolite. Three, never interrupt if the person you'd like to speak to is already engaged in another hallway conversation.

If my schedule allows, I leave for meetings ten minutes early so that I can pass the cubes and offices of people I need to get status or a deliverable from. This still constitutes a hallway conversation since I only poke my head in (keeping my feet firmly planted in the hallway). Again, never interrupt if they have someone in their cube or office, or if they are on the phone. And, don't stalk, hanging around waiting for someone to finish up. It makes people uncomfortable and looks like an act of desperation.

Walk the talk...

At least once a day, as my schedule will permit, I walk the floor for thirty or forty minutes, specifically dropping by to see my team members, a few executives, and others who, in one-way-or-the-other, make up the matrix of my initiatives. The goal is to try to stop by and visit everyone, personally, at least once a week.

I do not, repeat, do not ask for status. I keep the visit very informal. Why? No one wants to feel as if they are being micromanaged. Rather, I ask if there is anything I can do for them. The result is, they will on their own, without my prodding, provide me status. Quite often, it turns out that there are situations I can help them with that they might not have otherwise approached me on.

If someone has accomplished a major milestone, I thank them for their effort. The number one thing people need, even more than monetary reward, is recognition, to feel appreciated. Make this a priority. Bring it to the attention of others during status meetings, conference calls, etc. Never allow anyone to steal someone else's thunder. In fact, even if you, yourself, were instrumental in helping someone achieve success, you relinquish any credit.

Office decorum...

In the next few paragraphs, I'm going to address behaviors that might be seen as the "lesser evils" one can commit at work, but can have serious career consequences. The vast majority of successful people "look the part", do not curse, and are considerate of others. I dislike people who curse. Especially women in the workplace who think it makes them "one of the boys". It's vulgar and makes them sound like tramps. I have never been impressed or persuaded by the use of a curse word. If someone's vocabulary is so limited that the only way to emphasize their position is to curse, they're an idiot.

Now, on the flip-side, every now and then, in my own defense, I have cursed. But, it was by choice, not a "knee-jerk" reaction. Purposeful, targeted, and done rarely. Primarily used when putting idiots in their place.

Your little corner of the world...

Who doesn't enjoy the holidays? Christmas Day, the Fourth of July, and other holidays usually signify a day off from work for most people. For others, it brings out a perverse sense of "designer syndrome". These are the folks whose cubes or offices look like a display window from Saks Fifth Avenue. They think it's cute, festive...I have two words for these folks: *stop it*...leave the tinsel at home.

I have never seen an executive's office decorated for a

holiday. Based on this observation, there is only one conclusion I can draw: those who decorate *never* become executives. Get the picture? Don't misunderstand me; I enjoy the holidays tremens-dously; but I celebrate outside of work.

He said, she said...

Gossip is a career killer. Participating in "back-alley" conversations, innuendos, and half-truths will result in the "mark of Cain": "When you till the ground, it shall no longer yield its strength to you. A fugitive and a vagabond you shall be on the earth". - Genesis 4:12. You will become an outcast.

You don't have to be rude to others when they want to unload their little "juicy tidbits" about someone, just let them know you have no interest and leave it at that. We have a saying in the theater, "What goes around comes around". One day you might be the *gossiper*, the next, the *gossipy*.

Party like it's 1984...

Jingle Bells, Jingle Bells, Jingle all the way. 'Tis that time of year for the Christmas Party (I purposely didn't write Holiday Party...so sue me). Here are a few simple rules: do not get drunk; in fact, don't even get tipsy. Do not sit on anyone's lap, and don't allow anyone to sit on yours. If you can't dance, stay off the dance floor. If you can dance, keep it subtle. You are not auditioning for **Dancing with the Stars**.

If the day-to-day dress code is business casual, dress up, look polished. Give them an idea of just how good you might look sitting in a corner office. Have a few funny stories and jokes to share, appropriate for the occasion! Socialize, impress, thank those in leadership positions for a wonderful party and then ride off into the sunset leaving them wondering, "Who was that masked man (or woman)". Trust me; they'll know who you were (or inquire)!

It's all about the look...

When I think about "dress code", I can't help but think of the following song by ZZ Top:

Clean shirt, new shoes, and I don't know where I am goin' to.
Silk suit, black tie, I don't need a reason why.

They come runnin' just as fast as they can.
'Cos every girl crazy 'bout a sharp dressed man.

Okay, the idea is not to get anyone running, it's to get you noticed. As more and more companies allow workers to "dress down", that's all the more reason for you to "dress up". Some people come to work looking like complete slobs. This shows a lack of respect for themselves, as well as the company.

If you have no plans on moving up, then, by all means, continue to look like a bum. On the other hand, if you have aspirations, there is something to be said '*bout a sharp dressed man* (or woman). Consider the purchase of a suitable wardrobe an investment in your future...it will pay off handsomely (pun intended).

"When I was young, I thought as a child..."

Acting "age appropriate" on the job can be a challenge; especially if it's the business itself which fostered a "playhouse" atmosphere to start with. I got a call one evening from a friend who had been asked by a client to find an, "old f#%$^r. Someone who knows what they're doing".

Turns out, the client was a start-up *dot-com* of a major, established retailer. Their growth was extraordinary, and they were having difficulties keeping up with the very technologies they relied upon to maintain their success. When I arrived for the interview with the CEO and CIO, it was immediately apparent to me, that outside the three of us, no one else in the building appeared to be over the age of eighteen. After a brief conversation, I agreed to help resolve their situation.

While I hadn't noticed it on the day of my interview, the day I arrived to start work, something stood out. In front of the reception desk was the largest toy chest I'd ever seen. I watched as each employee who entered the building approached the toy chest and picked out their "toy for the day". I found this all quite amusing. And no, I didn't select a toy to play with. But, the toy chest was nothing in comparison to the funniest scene which repeated itself every time a meeting was called.

A large majority of the senior employees (probably nineteen years of age), drove little, electric cars around the office. While I would be patiently waiting in the conference room for the "kids" to assemble; the hallway would be a flurry of commotion. And, what was the reason for the mayhem? Well, apparently, there weren't enough *parking spaces* outside the conference room. Forcing some drivers to park quite a distance down the hallway; resulting in them having to walk. You can't make this stuff up. It should be noted that, at the end of the day, like all "good children", each employee did return their toy back to the toy chest before exiting the building.

While your home life might be in complete disarray, the office is where one needs to be organized, professional, and productive to succeed. If your career isn't progressing the way you would like it to, it's time to take the appropriate steps to "reap what you sow"...and keeping in mind that "sow" is the optimum word.

Chapter Eleven – "Just Once in a Lifetime"

Just once in a lifetime there's one special moment.

I handled my first negotiation when I was five years old. My Grandmother owned a deli and grocery store (with a soda fountain and penny candy counter) across the street from my kindergarten school in Paterson, New Jersey. After school, I would go to the store and wait for my mother so that we could walk home together. On my first day, my Grandmother assigned me the task of sweeping the floor. When I finished, I told my Grandmother that I had found some money while sweeping. Little did I know that she had "seeded" the floor with a few nickels, dimes, and pennies.

My Grandmother told me that since I had done such an excellent job, I could keep the money I found. She then asked me if I wanted to buy some candy with my money. I walked over to the candy counter and gazed at all the wonderful, assorted delicacies; wax lips and miniature wax soda bottles filled with a syrupy nectar, red, black, and brown licorice, fudge in little gold, tin cups with even littler gold, tin spoons to eat them with, chewing gums and bubble gums, jaw breakers, necklaces made of sweet tarts, and on and on....an endless array. Somehow, even at five, I knew instinctively that if I played my cards right, I could come out on top. After a few minutes, I looked up at my Grandmother and told her I was going to save my money. She smiled, told me what a "good boy" I was to save my money, and then told me to pick anything I wanted from the display case. I had my candy, I had my money. It didn't get any better than that. That was the *one-and-only* time that a negotiation went so smoothly. So, unless you're negotiating with *your* Grandmother, let's cover the basic ground rules you need to know in order to be a successful negotiator.

Last man standing (or woman)...

Here are the four basic rules of negotiating: one, if you don't know what you want from the deal, you have no business being at the table. Two, if you don't have a good idea of what's in it for the other side, you have no business being at the table. Three, when it comes to establishing the negotiated dollar amount, you never go first. And four, everyone needs to be a winner or else you will pay for this mistake in the long run.

Prior to any negotiation, you should have already detailed to the nth degree what benefits you will derive from going into business with the other party. If you wing it, you will lose. Next sucker. The same is true when it comes to understanding the benefits to be derived by the opposition. Research, research, research! Know who they are, what they've accomplished, where they've been, and where they're going. What was the catalyst that brought you both to the table in the first place? Did you approach them or did they approach you? This is important!

Negotiation is compromise. You need to know exactly what you would be willing to compromise on prior to the first meeting. Everyone is familiar with the classic example of a negotiation: You start at one-hundred, they start at zero...after going back and forth, you end at fifty. That is not negotiating. Not to be derogatory, but my ten year old niece could have handled that deal. The majority of people who don't handle negotiations think that money is always the primary focus. This is not true. While money is the ultimate goal in the majority of cases, the immediate benefit of two parties going into business with each other can be initially for other reasons.

For example, Company B is a start-up software development company and is trying to break into the Fortune 500 market. So far, they have been unable to penetrate the market because of the requirements many Fortune 500 companies have in regard to standard business practices; e.g. a company doing business must have annual revenues equal to or exceeding five million dollars; the business must be in practice for a minimum of three years, and so on. Company B does not meet any of these requirements; but landing a Fortune 500 contract is paramount to growing the business.

How would you handle the negotiations for Company B if

given the opportunity? How would you handle the negotiations if you were the Fortune 500 Company that was providing the opportunity to Company B? Are the wheels spinning?

I handle some aspect of a negotiation practically every day. Whether it's internal at the company I am consulting for, or dealing with outside vendors on their behalf. And, it doesn't end there. We all need to handle negotiations in our personal life, as well.

Nine years ago, I made a decision to build a small, private oasis in my backyard. Since my work seldom provides me time off, when an opportunity does present itself, I wanted to be able to relax without the headache of packing and traveling. Once the plans were completed by the architect, I invited three contractors out to the house to bid on the project. This period just so happened to be the *heyday* for contractors. Money was flowing, and they had more work than they could shake a stick at.

As the meetings progressed, each contractor's bid was higher than the last. Finally, with the third contractor, I started pulling and looking down at my shirt. Somewhat confused, the contractor asked what I was looking for. I replied, "I'm trying to find where on my shirt it says, Rockefeller!" They got the hint but wouldn't budge on their price. So, I rolled up the plans and put them in the closet. Three years later, the market for construction dried up. Again, I invited three contractors to bid on the project. This time, all three bids fell within my budget. I made my selection, and we broke ground that Spring. Two years later, it was completed (okay, you caught me...it was a little bigger than a small oasis). My friends affectionately call it, "Club Doug".

The point here is that sometimes there is no other choice but to walk away from a deal, no matter how much you may want to engage. There are moments that are "just wrong". Negotiations require patience and waiting until the moment is "just right".

Meet me halfway...

Friends of mine who work and are principles at one of the best Microsoft development companies in the world (offices throughout North and South America, Europe, the Middle East, and Asia Pac) recently had a situation. After developing a very unique "Windows Surface" application for a major hotel/resort chain, they failed to retain any of the rights to the application; a slight oversight.

The market for resale was huge; e.g. other resorts, the cruise industry, etc. How could the rights be reacquired after the fact? How could the current holder be persuaded to relinquish their rights? I was asked to resolve the situation. I stepped through the four basic rules and constructed my strategy. Then, I made the call. Four hours later, we came to an agreement and concluded our negotiation with a call to the Chairman of their company for final approval. Papers were drawn up and signed, resulting with my friends acquiring the rights for the resale of their application.

You may be asking yourself how this came about. First, rule one. I knew exactly what this deal meant to my friends. That was a "no brainier". The more important question was what could be offered that would be of interest to the hotel/resort chain? Remember that rule two requires research? While this was a very unique application, it wasn't even remotely a reason why someone would choose one hotel or resort over another. That was an important fact to keep in mind.

The hotel/resort chain paid two hundred fifty thousand dollars for the application, plus a three-year maintenance agreement; another seventy-five thousand dollars. Two other important facts to keep in mind; the application produced a product which was created and sold on-site to their guest (an impulsive purchase). Lastly, the hotel/resort had already begun asking for enhancements to the application soon after its initial implementation. All of the above were "key factors".

Next came the "math" (hang in here with me). The enhancements would cost an additional one hundred twenty-five thousand dollars. The yearly maintenance agreement was calculated at ten percent of the total application's price. Bundling the enhancements (which raised the application's cost to three hundred and seventy-five thousand dollars) and extending the maintenance agreement to five years would come to just over three hundred thousand dollars. For the hotel/resort chain, this would be the "carrot". The actual cost for development and support in providing the bundle totaled one hundred fifty thousand dollars. For the development company, this would be the "investment".

The retail product offered, via the application, had the potential to make over twenty-five thousand dollars per location, annually. This was another key factor in developing a strategy for resale.

You may be thinking, 'Wait a minute, you don't have the rights for resale, why are you considering this now?' Trust me; this isn't putting the cart before the horse. I need to know what the "breakeven" would be prior to my negotiating. If my friends could not make back their investment and be profitable, there was no sense in pursuing the deal. I constructed a "leasing" scenario for future sales.

The application, hardware, and maintenance would be bundled and offered at twenty thousand dollars on a two-year lease basis on a location-by-location basis (per resort, cruise ship, etc.). Note: there are several ways to construct a lease program which offers the best return and tax considerations to a customer. I am not going to cover those details here – let it suffice to say that the one I developed did.

Now, the resale offer was affordable, provided tax incentives and, within the lease period, would pay for itself and become a profit center. The breakeven? Ten customers; a drop in the bucket. I also worked up the "incentive" numbers for the hotel / resort chain, as well. The proposal took into consideration the buy-back of the modified proprietary rights, via the "bundled offer", consisting of the application enhancements and a five-year maintenance agreement at no cost, capital asset depreciation schedule, tax write-off considerations, and potential revenue.

This brings us to the difference between the sticker price, ticket price, perceived value, and net value. For this example, let's use a can of peas; an ingredient in chicken pot pies. The original sticker price was fifty-five cents a can. The sticker price is meaningless; meant to demonstrate how generous a discount was already applied when compared to the ticket price. It's an illusion. The ticket price was marked down to forty-nine cents a can.

Each consumer will have a different perceived value. Those who shop regularly at the big, discount supermarkets see the ticket price as high and a poor value. Those who shop regularly at the exclusive, boutique supermarkets see the ticket price as low and a good value. Whether or not a purchase is a "good deal" depends on factors beyond the cost. One must take into consideration any and all intrinsic value associated with the purchase, both tangible and intangible. The net value is your cost minus any benefit derived from the purchase. Your research showed that chicken pot pies, which contain peas, sell four times greater than chicken pot pies which do not contains peas.

This resulted in your applying a five percent reduction to the cost of the peas. The cost less t h e benefits derived of all the ingredients, less the sale of the pie, would be the net value. If your purchase of the peas resulted in a *minus* instead of a *plus* on the net value after selling the pie, you made a bad deal purchasing the peas. You should have negotiated a better price or waited until they had a two-for-one sale (for multiple pies). The bottom line, you *must*, I repeat, *must* walk away if a positive net value cannot be achieved during the negotiations.

Food for thought: Accounting principles aren't only important during a negotiation, they factor into just about everything we do; from balancing our personal check book to managing a multi-million dollar budget. It is important that you have at least a basic understanding of accounting: P&L, balance sheet, pro-forma projections, ROI, NPV COA, CAPEX, OPEX, etc. After all, if you're the person accountable for how the money is to be spent, you need to walk the talk (even if it's only baby-steps). Consider taking an Accounting 101 course at your local college.

Remember, I mentioned that the application would not be a factor in determining which hotel people would book? But, there was a certain prestige in exclusivity. I had to keep that in mind. I researched the individual locations of each property for the hotel/resort chain. I did the demographics on competitors, traveling distances, proximity to local airports, main highways, etc. Then, I drew a radius around each location based on the research: this became the "exclusivity zone".

Now, I had everything I needed to direct the negotiations in my favor. Almost. But, there was something I still needed to do. Timing is critical. If you are the one initiating the negotiations, you want to setup the initial meeting with no advance notice to the other party. The opposition should never be aware that there was any interest prior to your first call. Why? Think of the advantage of coming to the table already having done the required work with respect to rules one through four, while your opponent has not. While rule number three pertains to who will pull the trigger first to establish the "dollar amount", you should have already worked out where you need to be in this regard prior to any discussion. Having such an advantage is enormous. At the same time, should someone approach you first, you now know to push back the initial meeting date until you can complete your due diligence before coming to the table (if there's an interest).

Rule three (when it comes to establishing the negotiated dollar amount, you never go first) has many different aspects that need to be taken into consideration. Obviously, if you offer a product or service to a company, you will have to provide a dollar amount associated with your offering. This initial number is *not* the negotiated dollar amount. The typical approach would be to start "high" since, in this scenario, you only have one possible direction, and that's down. Now, it's time to wait for the other side to provide a number back. Be patient. Why would you revise your number prior to knowing their position? While you may have been willing to compromise a twenty-five percent discount, they might have been willing to do business at a ten percent discount. Once they do come back, then it's time to negotiate. It's very important that you have in your arsenal why your pricing is structured *as it is* to help substantiate your position.

If you are on the side of the table that's doing the purchasing, your goal is *not to get the lowest price.* Your goal is to get the *best product or service at the best price.* That's the distinction. If possible, open the proceeding to competitive bidding. Let all parties know that there are multiple players. This will be to your advantage. For example, if you are looking for new office space and it *must* have a specific address, this is single play negotiations. If, on the other hand, your office can be located within a five block radius of that address, this is multi-play negotiations.

With respect to revealing your hand (your bottom line), while in the paragraph above I told the provider to be patient and wait for the buyer to come back with a number, now I'm going to tell you to do just the opposite; force the provider to revise their number before you reveal your hand since the opposite could be said for the previous scenario. You may have been willing to accept only a ten percent discount while they may have been willing to offer a twenty-five percent discount. But you never would have known that if you showed your cards too soon.

How do you force your opponent's hand? By being subtle, e.g. "Have you considered what kind of discount you might be willing to offer if we could come to an agreement today?" I know a few poker players who think they're good negotiators. Negotiating and poker have no commonality whatsoever. While poker certainly does require skill, there is still the element of luck. I have yet to have anyone deal me four aces during a negotiation; I have in poker.

Once the proceedings start, and provided you are one hundred percent prepared, keep them going with as few breaks as possible and, if at all possible, conclude the negotiations on the same day. Why? Most people have little patience; so, use this tactic to your advantage. As people tire, they are more likely to concede and make concessions in your favor. A little more than two hours into the negotiations with the President of the Hotel/Resort chain, he made several suggestions to break and resume the discussion the following day. I would counter that I would be traveling and unavailable, and we should continue since we were so close to wrapping things up. When you have your opponent up against the ropes, this is the time to press, not retreat; keeping in mind that this is achieved through persuasion, not bullying.

Your approach needs to be positive and have the appearance of favoring the opposition. Rule four isn't a "maybe", it's an absolute and must be achieved. All parties involved in the negotiations need to come out as "winners". I have been a witness to idiots performing the exact opposite. They believe that being a "hard ass" and setting unrealistic demands demonstrates being a good negotiator. I recall one Vice President who, after a session ended and we were alone, stood up and told us all, "that's how you run a meeting. I had them quaking in their boots".

Seriously? First of all, the head of the company on the other side of the negotiations was someone who would never "quake". He just so happened to be the former CIO of the company he was pitching his idea to; us! Second, he was a very established businessman; worth millions, and had an exceptional reputation in the industry. Really now, do you think some young whipper-snapper, who was in a position "way over his head", was going to intimidate this gentleman? Shortly after I got back to my office, the former CIO called me. We had met, on many occasions, over the preceding year and worked on other deals, would have dinner when he was in town, and had established a good working relationship.

His first words were, "What got into that idiot, today?" I told him I saw the jackass eating cereal for breakfast. He must have been feeling his Wheaties. The bottom line, I suggested that the former CIO use his influence to go above the jackass' head so that we could finalize our negotiations; otherwise, it would never come to fruition. He did and was awarded the contract. He profited, and so did we. It was a win-win.

The win-win needs to be offered up during the proceedings. If the deal ends up being lopsided, both organizations will suffer. Why? Imagine you're negotiating with the start-up software development company mentioned in the beginning of this chapter. After several rounds of finalizing the dollar amount for the contract, your side insists that the price be below the industry average. After all, you're giving this start-up a great opportunity (and taking advantage of this fact). The start-up doesn't want to miss this opportunity, even though they know they can't deliver at that price, but accepts the offer. Now, imagine the outcome and the consequences for both parties. Not pretty. Both sides lose.

While the details in the final contract with the hotel/resort chain are proprietary and cannot be shared, you should have a good sense of how it was constructed; keeping in mind the *key factors*, the *carrot*, the *investment*, the *exclusivity zones*, and the *math*. The outcome of a negotiation should never be a surprise; not if you were prepared to direct and channel the talks to a pre-determined destination. And, just as we discussed in the chapter on sales-manship; once the deal is final, shut your mouth, shake hands, and leave the building.

Persuading others goes hand-in-hand with negotiating, from winning someone over to your way of thinking, up to asking for a raise. There are countless books on the art of persuasion. I recommend that you read one or two. A few points to keep in mind are:

- help the other side to conceptualize both the good and bad alternative endings to a situation you need their cooperation on.

- offer to help others, as an investment, so you can be in a position to call in your chips when you need their help.

- structure your conversation so that the second request is the objective. This way, when the response is "No" to the first request, respondents are more likely to say "Yes" to the second request so as not to appear unreasonable.

- people are more likely to agree with people they like. Make them smile, make them laugh.

- present your request as a collaboration, use *we* instead of *me*.

Negotiating a raise...

Everybody wants a raise. Who doesn't? The amazing thing is I have been told, repeatedly, that negotiating a raise is someone's "number one" fear on the job. Wanting and deserving are two entirely different things. When it comes to asking for a raise, making such a request should not even be considered unless you are in a position of strength. And only achievement equates to strength. Unfortunately, strength alone might not be enough. Employees are under certain constraints: salary caps based on the position, annual review metrics/bell curves, salary freezes, and on and on, all put it place to favor the company, not the worker. The only way to be paid what you are worth is to be worth a lot. It never hurts to ask. But before you go knocking on your Manager's door, make sure you can support your case, that you are a contributor to, and not a consumer of, the company's bottom-line.

Have you ever noticed that people are far better negotiating a deal for someone else than they are when it comes to negotiating a deal for themselves? Why? People tend to feel self-conscious and embarrassed about tooting their own horn. While it's easy for me to write, "Don't' be", it may not be that simple to overcome these feelings of insecurity. It's always easier to make a deal when you "hold all the marbles", but it's entirely different when the other side has all the power. So, before one can even consider making a deal, one must be confident that their proposition has merit.

A "dress rehearsal" is an excellent confidence builder and can be quite illuminating. Take the time to list every conceivable point of contention the other side can present; e.g. "This really isn't a good time to be asking for a raise. I'm sure you're aware that the company lost money the last three quarters." or "If I give you a raise, I'd have to give everyone a raise." The examples above have absolutely no bearing on whether you are deserving of a raise or not. They're fodder. So, how does one combat such arbitrary nonsense? Your arsenal needs to be stock-piled with accomplishments; your contributions, your commitment and loyalty to the company, your attention to detail, your going above and beyond, when necessary. Perhaps the company's bottom line would have been far worse without your contributions. You are not everyone else. Perhaps the rest don't deserve a raise; but you do!

The important thing to remember during any negotiation is not to get flustered. Remain calm. "Never let'em see you sweat." This is not always an easy thing to do; not where passion is concerned. And, people do get passionate when it comes to their positions and beliefs.

Whenever I have been in a heated debate and the proceeding has reached an impasse, I implement a moratorium; a brief separation for each side to confer amongst themselves. Then, when both sides regroup, the first thing I remind them of is, while we are still very far apart from where we need to be, I believe we can work through our differences and come to a mutual agreement which will satisfy both our positions. But before we resume, there is one question each side needs to answer; do you want to be here? Is this deal still something both sides want? Because, if the answer is "No" by one or the other or both parties; then we should part company and go our separate ways!

This serves several purposes: one, it reminds people why we got together in the first place. What was it that made the prospect of doing business with each other so promising to begin with? Two, if during the proceedings either side came to the conclusion that they no longer want to do business with the other, it's best just to end it right here and now and move on. Three, if both sides believe that the deal is still in everyone's best interest, it's time to stop bickering and find the commonality that will finalize the negotiations.

Tit for tat...

Bartering is a great way to get goods or services with little or no outlay of cash. It still takes negotiation skills not to get fleeced during the proceedings. Research is very important. If you have no idea of the value of what is being offered by the other side, how can you make a comparison to what your side is offering in return? I could very easily tell you that the stick I'm holding in my hand (which, by the way, came from my backyard) is valued at ten thousand dollars. In return, I want ten thousand dollars worth of widgets from you. Are you going to take my word for it? Hardly. Whether you are the one initiating the barter or the one being approached, as with any negotiation, you need to know precisely what the benefits for both parties are before entering into a deal.

I've initiated many barter deals while getting my start-up companies off the ground. In the beginning, cash is usually hard to come by and, what little there may be, needs to be held onto for dear life. An exchange of corporate stock for goods or services is the solution. Two benefits are: When acquiring goods at no cost, you've just increased the company's "bottom line" with the acquisition of assets; and for services, while they don't increase the company's "bottom line", do help to move the company forward, which is just as important. Legal and accounting services are two, in particular, that are worth noting.

Here is how I typically structure a deal. The initial par value of the corporate common stock is valued at a $.01 per share. A total of one million shares are issued, which I purchase fifty-one percent of the company for $5,100 (a controlling interest). The corporation pays for the balance of the issued stock (four hundred ninety thousand shares) and holds the remaining stock in reserve. The reserved stock is then priced for the next group of investors at $1.00 per share ($490,000). The reserved stock can be issued for any combination of cash, goods, or services.

Like most start-ups, I'm in need of computers, a phone system, a copier, and every other conceivable piece of office equipment and furniture. Luckily, you just happen to be the proprietor of a retail establishment that carries everything I need. I pay you a visit. I'm not shy. But, before I walked through your doors, I did my homework. I know the standard industry pricing, both sticker and ticket, for every item I'm interested in. I also researched what the typical costs were for an establishment in your line of business for each and every item.

Let's use a copier as our example. You paid your supplier $1,000 for the Model Q2000 displayed in your showroom. Your sticker price is $4,250 and has a marked down ticket price of $2,500. An annual maintenance and service contract is 10% of the ticket price, or $250 a year.

After I've introduced myself and explained my company and

the enormous potential it represents for you as an investor, we get down to the numbers. As an inducement, I offer stock in exchange for the copier based on its sticker price, not the ticket price. I know you paid $1,000 for the copier while I'm offering $4,250 in stock. I also know that maintenance and service contracts have high profit margins. I therefore offer an additional $750 in stock for a three-year contract. The offer now stands at $5,000 in company stock for $1,300 in business cost (the copier plus cost to fulfill a service contract).

You're interested, but you have reservations. What if my company doesn't make it? I was prepared for that. Should my company go under, your business would be able to write off the loss at the acquired stock value. Taking into account that your business pays the standard 36% in corporate taxes; a write off of $5,000 at 36% would equate to $1,800. This is $500 over your original cash outlay for the Model Q2000 and three years of service. Now you have nothing to lose. And, should my company grow and the value of its stock increase, you could realize a substantial profit. It's a win-win.

If you ever intend to start a business, your skills to negotiate, barter, and persuade will be key factors in your being successful. If you're a novice, start practicing on your friends and family. A piece of advice, your energies should be concentrated on researching and writing a solid business plan which can entice prospective investors. I've known a few folks who thought they were entrepreneurs but, in reality, weren't even close. Any time you meet someone who spends more time figuring out what their company name is going to *sound like* and what their business card is going to *look like* than how the business is going to achieve its goals; run, don't walk, to the nearest exit.

Remember, negotiating isn't an evil, it's the norm. People want and need to do business with each other every day. The objective is not to *crush* the other side; save that for your *competition*; not a prospective *partner*. Do your homework, always be reasonable and know where, how, and what you can compromise on to meet each other's objectives. Successful negotiations are an acquired skill. Practice and learn from your mistakes.

Always be willing to listen to what the opposite side may suggest. Many times, *great ideas* are presented by the opposition;

ideas your side of the table will not have thought of. Adopting and conforming to another's ideas can be the difference between a successful deal and one that "goes south". Last thought, if you have children and they constantly get their way, do not take a position where your negotiation skills are essential to your role in the organization. This would not be a smart career move.

Chapter Twelve – "The Long and Winding Road"

Don't keep me waiting here; lead me to your door.

Leaders aren't *made*, Leaders are *born*. While there are many who will disagree with me, from my perspective, it's a cold, hard fact. And, I don't mean born in the sense that Leaders emerge from the womb as a pint-size version of General Patton, riding crop, pearl-handled pistols and all, barking out orders. It's a combination of environment, upbringing, and the individual spirit; the right ingredients in the right proportions. One could take a thousand individuals who never had exposure to the afore-mentioned prerequisites, place them in a so called intensive "leadership program", and not one will emerge as a true Leader. Some may become better Managers, Supervisors, or the like, but none will emerge as a Leader. Leadership is instinctive, not something that is taught. Leaders come in three flavors...good, bad, and mediocre; from Abraham Lincoln to Adolf Hitler, and in between. And then there are the pseudo-Leaders...inept idiots posing as Leaders. These are the ones you need to keep your eyes on.

Leadership is not management. The Manager's job is to plan, organize, and coordinate. The Leader's job is to share a vision, to inspire, and to motivate. Can a Leader be a good Manager? Absolutely! Can a Manager be a good Leader? Maybe; that de-pends on whether or not the Manager had the innate characteristics of leadership to begin with. True Leaders don't falsify, pseudo-Leaders do. I've witnessed, on more than one occasion, Managers under the guise of leadership attempting to manufacture a "Kumbaya" moment. It never works.

A Leader helps to set the wheels in motion. A Leader will steer and grease the wheels now and then, if they squeak. But, such moments need to follow a natural progression. They don't come off an assembly line. Today, management has a much different approach than it did in the past. The days of management ruling with an "iron fist" are long over. An end to an era so *eloquently* phrased in the song, **Take This Job and Shove It**. I've known and worked with some exceptional Managers over the years. While they are not Leaders, their managerial abilities have contributed to my leadership positions being successful. I am very grateful.

"I will follow you"...

Leaders inspire. Leaders influence. Leaders instill confidence. Leaders foster creativity and ingenuity. Are you familiar with the story of little Johnny? On Johnny's second day in Kindergarten, the teacher announced that the class was going to finger-paint. Johnny immediately imagined all sorts of things to paint. 'I could paint a fire engine', he thought to himself. 'No, wait...maybe a tiger or even a big boat'. Then the teacher said, "And today, class, we're going to finger-paint a *flower*". Johnny immediately revised his thinking. 'Okay, a flower. But there are so many to pick from. Which one, which one?', as he pictured dozens of flowers in his head. Again, the teacher addressed the class, "And, the flower we're going to paint today is a *daisy*." Johnny, always a quick thinker, pictured a daisy painted the color of the rainbow. It would be awesome. "And our daisy", said the teacher, "is going to have a green stem and leaves with a white flower on the top". And so the class began to paint.

Not that many weeks later, Johnny's father got a transfer to a new city in another state. On Johnny's first day with his new classmates, the teacher announced that the class was going to finger-paint. Immediately, all the kids around him were scurrying for supplies, going back to their desk, and started painting. The teacher noticed that Johnny just sat there. The teacher walked over to him and said, "Johnny, why haven't you joined the other children?" Johnny looked up at the teacher and replied, "You didn't tell us what to paint". Smiling, the teacher said, "You can paint anything you want. It's up to you". Johnny got his supplies, joined the other children, and started to paint. When Johnny finished, he handed the teacher his painting. It was a daisy with a green stem and leaves with a white flower on the top.

I was fortunate to have people who influenced my life who were very much like the second teacher in the story. Foremost were my parents. Mom was a very creative person; into the arts and music, as well as a born Leader. Holidays were always exceptional and exciting because of Mom. I remember one particular night when I was nine, Mom and I were wrapping gifts for our aunts, uncles, and cousins. When we finished, there was a large box, several small boxes, and about a dozen empty wrapping paper tubes on the table. She looked at me and said, "You want to make a Christmas castle?" Mom and I stayed up until almost two in the morning working on the castle. When we were done, it was the most amazing thing I had ever seen.

The smaller boxes were cut and positioned on top of the larger box to form the main castle with its many parapets; all covered and layered in silver and gold wrapping paper. The tubes, of varying widths and heights, were fastened against the main castle with clasps. They, too, were wrapped in various color papers; reds, blues, purples, etc. Cones were shaped from paper and trimmed with zigzag border and positioned on top of each tube. Glitter and rhinestones were added; the entranceway was cut out and hung down to the table with wrapping string forming the drawbridge cables. Windows were cut out and covered with transparent paper from the inside.

Even as I write and describe what we did, no words can paint a picture of how fantastic and beautiful the Christmas castle looked when we were done. That castle became the center piece on the dining room table for many years; year after year, bringing back that wonderful memory of the night Mom made me feel so special, so loved. Something she did quite often for all her children.

Dad's approach was a little different. When I was fourteen, Dad decided it was time to remodel the bathroom. As he and I stood there in the bathroom, he looked at me and said, "Well, what do you think? What do you think we should do?" Now, remember, I mentioned earlier that my father was a Mechanical Engineer, a draftsman. There was no way that my father didn't already have this remodeling planned and designed down to the last detail. But that never popped into my head. Instead, I gave my father my ideas. My father listened as I went on about how I would do this and that and that and this. When I was finally finished, my father said, "Some good ideas there. Let's try it your way".

And, that's how we proceeded with the project. I am positive that some of my ideas were out-and-out crazy. Come on, I was fourteen! And now, when I think back, I faintly recall hearing the sound of electric construction tools humming in the background while I dozed off for the night after a hard day's work with Dad. I'm sure Dad was disassembling and reassembling some of my *great* ideas. But, he never said anything. Rather, he made us partners in the project. Equal say. Equal responsibility. He built my confidence in myself, tremendously. He always did and eventually, I did have some *great* ideas and the confidence to implement them.

"Put it off until tomorrow"...

We all have money-making ideas. But, very few people put them into action. Some of my friends have come up with "sure winners" but sat on them for years until someone else had the same idea and implemented it. Remember the saying, "the only thing that's new, is what's new to you". Many people all share similar ideas each and every day. It's those who act first and go to market who reap the rewards for their effort.

One example of how easy it is to make money in this great country of ours was when I was dating a girl who worked for a National Historic Museum. After a private tour, we ended up at the gift shop. I immediately noticed that one of the greatest inventions for which the museum was established was not on display for sale. I asked why? She didn't know. So, we approached the curator and asked. The answer was simple. No one had ever offered a replica of that particular product to be sold in the gift shop. The next question was obvious. So, I asked, how does one sell a souvenir to a National Historic Museum?

It involved three simple tasks. The next day, I tackled task one. I went into New York City to the import/export district and visited six businesses. Each had several miniatures of the specific product I was looking for. But, which was an exact replica? I purchased a dozen samples and headed home. After a little research, the match was identified.

After completing the next two tasks (notice that I am not sharing...after all, if you are interested in pursuing something similar, I've already given you the starting point…show some initiative!), I received a letter of authorization from the United States Department of the Interior that I could sell my product to the museum. I paid twenty cents per product, sold it to the museum for two dollars and ninety-five cents, and they sold it to the public for four dollars and ninety-five cents. With very little effort, money was rolling in, month after month. And mind you, for many months, it was the number one selling souvenir in the gift shop.

This is what Leaders do. Leaders don't procrastinate. I personally believe procrastination is the number one reason why people are not successful at work or in life. Taking the initiative to put "thought into action" takes a serious commitment; being obligated. Many shun what they perceive to be a disagreeable task. In fact, in a majority of cases, the procrastinator has overblown, in their mind's eye, the effort required to such an extent that they've made the task appear even more unpleasant than it is.

Are things piling up at work and around the house? Is every conceivable excuse being made not to tackle what needs to be done? This is a serious problem. Why are some folks like this? Are they just lazy? Do they lack self-confidence? Writing this book is a good example. I wrote the book at night and on the weekends. There were many times I was tired after an exhausting day cleaning up a "big mess" for a client. But, if the book was to be finished, it required commitment. There were days where the words flowed onto the page; I couldn't type fast enough. And then, there were those days where I'd work and re-work a paragraph or two for what seemed like an eternity. It reminded me of the famous quote by Dorothy Parker, "I hate writing but love having written".

Day in and day out, what has always kept me going is seeing the difference, the contribution, the progress my hard work has made in my life. In my mind's eye, I have always seen each and every task that presents itself as a challenge; an opportunity to learn, to build character. I remember deciding I was going to scrub the deck one morning. I filled up a bucket with warm water, added some bleach, and went to one end and started. After a few minutes, a two-by-two foot patch was cleaned and rinsed. I stood there being very proud of myself; the deck looked brand new. Then, I turned around and realized how much more of the deck remained. The far end of the deck appeared to be in another state (I think it was Wisconsin); the deck totaled just over twelve-hundred square feet. I think my initial thought was, 'What possessed me to start this?' But, it needed to be done. I could have given up. I could have contracted someone to finish the job. I did neither.

Rather, I stopped looking back over my shoulder to see what still *remained* and concentrated on looking in front of me on what had been *accomplished*. Several hours later, the deck cleaning was finished and looked great (mind you, better than any contractor would have done...after all, this was my house). If one is incapable of doing the disagreeable; of rolling up their sleeves and "getting it done", they will never be successful. Period!

"You say tomato, I say tomahto"...

Leaders are in concrete. Leaders are the cornerstone of an organization. At least, that needs to be the *appearance* to those being lead. The team needs direction. Nothing is worse than a Leader who appears unsure of him or herself. What the team doesn't need to know is that the concrete hasn't set; that it is still pliable; allowing the Leader flexibility. People need to be lead. It's human nature. The vast majority will relinquish the responsibility of leading, only because of the effort it takes to do so, and will gladly follow someone else's lead; for good or bad.

Leaders listen carefully. Leaders weigh the importance of what others are sharing with them. That's why the concrete only has the appearance of stone. Flip-flopping will have disastrous results. One-directional focus is critical. When others sufficiently persuade and convince me that a course correction is necessary, I make the navigational adjustment immediately, without fanfare. Once embarked on the new course, I am as in concrete as I was on the old compass-point; keeping the team focused.

One summer, I hired a college intern to work for my computer-based marketing company. I wanted to do my share to help the next generation. The student was a marketing major who just completed his junior year. One morning, there was a knock outside my office door, when I looked up, the intern was standing in the doorway holding a four-foot-wide by three-foot-high map of the United States. I asked how I could help him. He entered my office, enthusiastically, telling me how he had worked all night devising a marketing strategy for my company. The intern then stood the large map on my desk. Located across the map were hundreds and hundreds of little, round-topped, colored pins. I remember my first impression being how uniformly straight up-and-down the pins had been positioned. I could see why it took him all night. The intern then went on to explain what the colored pins represented, why they were positioned where they were, and on and on and on. I sat there and listened to every word.

When he finished, he asked me what I thought of his strategy. It was quite obvious he was very pleased with his presentation; he was grinning from ear-to-ear. My initial thought was, 'Here's someone who played the board game **Risk** one too many times!' I couldn't shake the thought of comparing his strategy to the Allies' invasion at Normandy. I thought back to how my father helped me foster confidence in myself. Like my Dad, I told him there were some good ideas and that I'd like to set up some time to review his strategy in greater detail. Why would I take the time if his plan was so "off the mark"? Surely, I had better things to do with my time. But, wasn't this the very reason I on-boarded an intern; to teach, to mentor?

During our subsequent meetings over the remainder of the summer, I instructed him on the "real world" implementation of a marketing strategy as opposed to what is taught in a college class-room and textbooks. I hadn't thought about that day for a long time. Now that I have, my hope is that this young gentleman, after graduation, went on to devise some of the greatest marketing campaigns known to man. Would be nice.

"War, what is it good for?"...

From time to time, Leaders need to settle disputes. While we may not possess the Wisdom of Solomon, a Leader needs to act immediately and act fairly to maintain the peace. Before I bring any of the parties involved in a dispute together, I meet with them individually. This serves two purposes. First, people are more likely to reveal discrepancies when talking one-on-one. This is why the police place suspects into separate interrogation rooms. Now, don't get ahead of me here. No one is interrogating anyone at the office. It was just a reference. Pay no attention to that bright lamp in my office.

The second reason is so I can devise a strategy for when the ad-versaries are brought back together for a face-to-face. By hearing each side of the story, I have a strong sense of who was right and who was wrong. This is where the previous chapter on perception comes into play. That knowledge determines the order I will let them speak. This is very important. It also helps me to formulate my questions and comments for the meeting, as well as specifically who I will address them to and in what sequence. Again, very important. If the arbitration is structured properly, the adversaries will "see the light" and come to an agreement seemingly on their own.

Leaders never reprimand someone in public. Never. This is why the "door" was invented. Get behind one when you need to correct someone's behavior. The most harmful and debilitating action one person can do to another is to embarrass or humiliate them in public. Such scarring does not heal quickly. Back when I was younger, the only times I would become enraged were those situations where I was publicly embarrassed. I would immediately retaliate with no regard to any potential consequence for my actions. Nowadays, I'll just tell you to go "shove it!" Be considerate of your fellow co-workers, even if someone is provoking you and doing their best to entice and bait you into an exchange. Pass up the offer.

"It's too late to apologize"...

Mistakes will define your character. We all make them. It's how you "own up" that will set you apart and define your character. Leaders do not implement a cover-up or lay the blame on someone else. Leaders "step in front of the bus". There is no single, greater act a Leader can perform to earn the respect and loyalty of those they lead than that of "the defender". Success requires taking risks. If a Leader has not instilled the confidence in those they lead to attempt and fail without fear of reprisal, no one will innovate.

There is a well-known quote from Thomas Edison when he was asked about his many failures while inventing the light bulb. Edison reportedly said, "I have not *failed* one thousand times; I have *successfully* discovered one thousand ways *not* to make a light bulb". But, what many might not know is that Edison shared his perspective, that *each failure was a success*, with all of his employees from the *very first failure*. While disappointment and set-backs are common occurrences in most pursuits, Leaders encourage. To quote Winston Churchill, "Success consists of going from failure to failure without the loss of enthusiasm". Leaders keep the momentum going; especially during those times where others might throw in the towel.

The important thing about mistakes is to learn from them. I made a few doozies during my career. Early on at the private bank where I was consulting, the business Leaders for a major initiative stopped by my cube. The system being developed needed a user to log on to four separate systems; the OS2 desktop, the Novell network, Rack F (the mainframe email application), and IBM's CICS middleware authorization, for the bank application. Single sign-on, at that time, was unheard of. A user would have to log onto each system, one at time, as each logon screen popped up. The business very much wanted to have this headache go away. I had been asked to do just that.

The Senior Vice President, along with a few other business executives, had stopped by to see how things were progressing. The Senior Vice President of Systems, who we'll call Harry, just happened to be passing my cube and overheard me telling the business executives that I was very close to a solution. Suddenly, my phone rang. It was Harry. He instructed me to "politely" tell the business Leaders that there was a situation that required my immediate attention and to wrap up my conversation with them and then come down to his office. I did as instructed. When I entered Harry's office, he asked me to close the door and to have a seat.

Harry then told me "just how things were done at the bank". Harry went on to say, "It's great that you're close to having a solu-tion, but we never, never share anything with the business until we've talked amongst ourselves and established a price". What I didn't know was that solutions were *sold* to the business; not provided gratis. Harry instructed me to inform the business that I had run into some stumbling blocks and that it was going to take longer than anticipated, if successful at all. Although I completed the single sign-on approach the following day, it wasn't offered to the business for almost another two months. By then, the negotiated price for the solution was worked out and then it was implement. The cost to the business: two million dollars. I learned from my mistake and followed the prescribed way of doing business from that day on.

It should be noted that Harry spoke to me in a calm manner. He knew I was new to the organization and didn't know the ropes. Harry could have chewed the hell out of me but didn't. He was a smart man, a good Leader, and someone who, over the years, I came to respect. The majority of us, when we do make a mistake, are as much upset with ourselves as those our mistake may have impacted. A good Manager or Leader will not exacerbate the situation in an attempt to make those who perpetrated the error feel even worse. Then again, for someone who is incapable of owning up to their mistakes, learning from them and then moving on, this will be a problem. Judge accordingly and then take the appropriate steps.

Unfortunately, some people on the job will inherit their bad behavior from others. I recall a day when the business sponsor for a project asked me to come down to his office. When I entered, he showed me an email he had constructed and was about to send off to both IT and Business Leaders. I knew this project very well, as it fell directly under my auspices. The email was a scalding, torrential rampage on the project team's failure to meet the business' deadline; mind you a deadline the business self-imposed and had no basis in reality. The email was completely and utterly undeserving. I knew this particular Manager's boss. His boss was ruthless; known throughout the organization as a tyrant. Over time, the business sponsor was now emulating the idiot he reported into. Not a smart move. The thing is, I liked this guy. He had a lot of great qualities.

Never one to mince words (most of you know me by now), I told him straight-up that sending the email would not be a smart move. One, being demanding and unreasonable served no purpose outside of creating friction. Two, the development team had worked their butts off to meet a very unrealistic date and would complete the application in a relatively short period of time. And, three, if anything, he should be sending out an email thanking everyone for their extraordinary effort and his sincerest appreciation for a job well done. I told him that this would not only boost the team's morale, it would earn him their respect. He looked at me and said, "I don't know. I've got to think about it". As I was leaving his office, I turned around and said, "Do what you *know* is right. Not what you *think* is right".

That afternoon, an email was sent to the project team, with IT and Business Leaders copied, thanking them for their extraordinary effort and their commitment to the project. If the original email, which reprimanded the project team, had been sent, it would have been a disaster. The reconstructed email had the results I predicted. The website successfully completed in a relatively short period of time. The site was developed for a little under three hundred thousand dollars and sold to a major cable television company for millions. It should be noted that the business sponsor moved up in the organization, while his tyrant of a boss was let go.

On the lighter side on making a mistake, one of my best friends landed his first job after high school at the largest, electric provider in the state. His first assignment was to install shelving into their fleet of vans. After a few hours on the job, the shop supervisor asked where the puddle of gasoline he was standing in was coming from. My friend looked up and said, "From the hole I just drilled in the gas tank.".

My friend made a mistake. He didn't try to make excuses. He owned up. My friend went on to get his degree (courtesy of the company) in *nuclear engineering* and work for the company for forty-two years until his retirement. We should all feel a sense of relief that, at no other time, after his first day was he ever again asked to drill into anything. As an added benefit, after working all those years in the nuclear division, my friend now "glows". We use him, occasionally, as a night light.

"I can see clearly, now"...

A great line from the movie, **The Titans** is: "Attitude reflects leadership". My addition, "Confidence reflects attitude". A Leader must continually demonstrate confidence in their ability to succeed. An attitude nothing short of "there is no alternative to success". I have observed, in more recent years, that the younger generation lacks stamina. Many are quick to give up or give in when it comes down to crunch time. They're soft and undisciplined. I truly believe that military service should be mandatory for every student right out of high school.

I think back to the day our platoon went on a twenty-mile forced march with full gear and rifle in hand. About ten miles in, a soldier collapsed. It was made immediately clear by the drill sergeant that, as platoon leader, it was my responsibility to handle the situation. He wasn't offering up any advice. It didn't take more than a second or two to realize what needed to be done.

First, I checked to see if first aid needed to be administered to the soldier. It didn't. Second, I then divvied up the "downed" soldier's gear and rifle among the four Squad Leaders at the head of each squad line. I gave them instructions that they were to pass the equipment to the next soldier down the line for each remaining mile until the march was completed. Third, myself and another soldier I selected (the biggest guy in the outfit), helped to get the collapsed soldier to his feet and then draped his arms around our necks; with me on the right and the big guy on the left. With our support, he was able to walk. We lost some time, but we didn't lose a man. The platoon worked as a team and evenly shared the responsibility in "righting" the situation. No one complained. It was our job. It's what we signed up for.

Leadership requires discipline. Clear thinking and physical stamina are achieved by exercising both the mind and the body. The saying, "everything in moderation", is not necessarily good advice. Some things in moderation can ruin you, or even worse, kill you. I've never done drugs; never, not even once. I took a lot of heat for that growing up; especially considering it was the era of Woodstock and Haight-Ashbury. But, I was never one to succumb to peer-pressure. I'd just tell you to "go to hell". Back then, many of my friends did drugs and, to bust me, when saying my name "Douglas", would pronounce it "Drugless".

I exercise, eat right, avoid both fried foods and fast foods, take my vitamins, and have a drink, occasionally. I like whiskey and soda. I don't have high blood pressure or high cholesterol. I don't have low-T or prostate problems. I'm not on any medications. Even though I don't have to, I do much of my own yard work. My wife and I maintain our own household. We aren't couch potatoes. We like outdoor activities; hiking, shooting, swimming, to name a few.

I'm not relaying all of this as if to say "look at me", rather it's to say "look at you". God willing, both you and I will get to stick around for a while longer. Your mental and physical health requires being disciplined. If you're not, your enjoyment while you're here on planet Earth will be diminished. It's never too late to improve oneself. Go ahead; your family and friends "got your back".

"God Bless America"...

It is my suggestion that you be involved in *your* community, *your* schools, and *your* government. The key word here is *"your"*. Our institutions need leadership. If you have what it takes to lead, pick up the gauntlet and please do so. If you're not a Leader; become a participant. Get involved! Too many people leave it to others and then complain when things don't turn out quite like they had hoped they would. In the vernacular of the street, "Hope ain't gonna cut it, Jack"!

Be informed. Do not rely on the internet as your one and only source for current events. The internet is a cesspool of lies, rumors, hate rhetoric, and innuendos. For me, personally, I read several newspapers and watch several television broadcasts o get a general consensus across multiple perspectives; this is very important. Do not pigeon hole yourself into one ideology. Having a well-rounded view will serve you well and help considerably in your decision making process in every aspect of life, not just politics. Always find out as much as you can pertaining to both sides of an issue. Why?

Between those two points of view lies the truth. If one is fearful of hearing both sides of an argument or position, you are an ideologue; and as such, will make "wrong" decisions. The more informed you are, the more choices are available to base your decision on. Isn't that better than being somebody's parrot and touting the "party line" when it's indefensible?

"A promise made is a promise kept"...

Are you someone who lives up to their *word*; who honors their commitments, promises and obligations? I truly hope so. Nothing in life, I repeat, nothing will define *who you are* to others more than your *word*. Commitments, promises and obligations are not maybes...they're absolutes.

I have known many people throughout my lifetime who haven't shared my perspective on this subject. They repeatedly fail to meet their *commitments, promises and obligations*. Now, any future utterance out of their mouths rings hollow. Why? It's a matter of trust. As the old proverb goes: "Fool me once, shame on you. Fool me twice, shame on me."

I recall a story my mother told me about my Grandmother. One day a neighbor came to visit my Grandmother at her grocery store. The woman told my Grandmother that her family had fallen on hard times and asked if she could borrow twenty dollars. It was the time of the Great Depression and twenty dollars was a very large sum of money.

My Grandmother went into the backroom and returned carrying a cookie jar. When she opened it, a twenty dollar bill was inside. She then handed the money to the neighbor with her hope that the family's situation would improve. The women expressed her gratitude, and told my Grandmother that she would repay the debt as soon as the family was able to.

Almost a year later, to the day, the neighbor came back into the store. My Grandmother had not seen her once in all that time, but was happy to see her again, and ask how the family was. The women explained that her family was again having difficulty, and asked if she could borrow twenty dollars.

My Grandmother, as she did before, went into the backroom and returned with the cookie jar. When she opened it, it was empty. My Grandmother then looked at the neighbor and said, "It's a shame you hadn't paid back the twenty dollars you borrowed. If you had, it would have been here for you to borrow again." My Grandmother was one smart cookie.

Each of us will see our own reflection in the mirror at least once a day. Do you like who you see looking back? Be someone others can place their trust in. There's no greater feeling than having *earned* the respect of others.

"Different strokes for different folks"....

I'd like to take a moment to speak to those senior Leaders who presently have the authority to create and maintain their corporate culture, and to those future Leaders who will eventually inherit this responsibility: *Stop treating your consultants as second class citizens!* It is despicable. I have consulted at corporations where consultants were afforded every amenity provided to their full-time employees; e.g. invited to Town Hall meetings and ice cream socials, the annual summer picnic and the Christmas party; monthly award ceremonies, etc.

Then, there are those corporations who purposely segregate

consultants from the populace. Their prevailing attitude is: "They're not really one of us. We just need them to do whatever it is we brought them in to do and then leave". Such an attitude erodes the very foundation of team building. Companies with a "snob mentality" often have more difficulties fostering cooperation and commitment among their ranks; resulting in a greater percentage of failed initiatives. Leaders are not segregationists, Leaders are unifiers! Be one!

And, while we're on the topic of consideration, it would be nice if the heads of Corporate America would show greater respect to those they employ who have served in the military. Less than three percent of Americans have served this great nation. Why aren't employers providing Veterans Day as a paid holiday for the few who provided the freedom they now enjoy? It wouldn't be all that difficult. Request each veteran to provide a copy of their DD214 so it can be on file. Those registered vets (whether an employee or a consultant) get a paid holiday; everyone else doesn't. If any non-vet in an organization complains, tell them you'd be only too happy to give them the day off, too. Tell them all they need to do is: Enlist, serve honorably, and bring back a copy of their DD214. Otherwise, tell them to shut up! It's that simple.

Postscript on Leadership: Today, April 11, 2013, the Medal of Honor was awarded to U.S. Army Chaplain Emil J. Kapaun. What a remarkable man. I was deeply moved by the ceremony as I listened to the story of his heroism and bravery. Few of us will ever possess the courage of Emil Kapaun. Chaplain Kapaun's actions "remind us of the good we can do each and every day, regardless of the most difficult of circumstances". Please take a moment to search the web to read his story. This is a great lesson in leadership and humility we all can learn from.

God bless you, Chaplain.

Chapter Thirteen – "Make 'em Laugh"

Make 'em laugh, make 'em laugh. Don't you know everyone wants to laugh?

Having a sense of humor and applying it to the absurdity that often surrounds us is key; at least from my take on the world. Unfortunately, much of today's humor is vulgar; absent of repartee. When did "wit" go out of vogue? Rather, cursing, toilet humor, and cruelty are offered up in countless movies, television shows, commercials, and stand-up routines. How many times is some idiot writer or comic going to resort to flatulence as their "go to" shtick? It's even found its way into Disney movies. Please, don't misunderstand me. I love a good joke as much as anyone and am, quite often, the joke teller at most gatherings. I enjoy making people laugh. But, I always take into consideration who my audience is. There is a time and a place for telling *adult* jokes. The workplace is not one of them. Around youngsters is another. Always act appropriately.

I have my heroes when it comes to the *who's who* where "funny" is concerned. One was Johnny Carson. Johnny was not only an amazing quick wit; he was an extraordinary host and interviewer. His combined skills and warm personality endeared him to a nation for decades. Here's...to you, Johnny!

My favorite playwrights are first and foremost George S. Kaufman and Moss Hart. Many of you may be saying, who? Yes, these gentlemen go back a ways. Even before my time. But as "the" example of how to write a funny play, they were the epitome of funny. Their plays (and later movies) of **You Can't Take It With You**, **Once in a Lifetime**, **The Man Who Came To Dinner**, **Stage Door** (co-authored with Dorothy Parker), **Animal Crackers, The Coconuts** (written for the Marx Bros. and co-authored with Morrie Ryskind) and many others scripts filled playhouses and movie theaters with laughter. In more recent times, there are the great comedies of Neil Simon and Mel Brooks, and the movies of Woody Allen. A little further back was George Bernard Shaw, and even further back, Jonathan Swift and Miguel de Cervantes (should you enjoy satire, as I do). For me, there has been a dirge in true comic writing. Nowadays, I find very little to laugh at when attending a movie, a stage play, or surfing channels on the small screen.

A few "tricks of the trade" when writing comedy are the time elapse and the aside (in theater) or breaking the Fourth Wall (in film). The time elapse is just what it sounds like. The "setup" takes place early on in the story. Then, once an audience has completely forgotten about the "setup", the punch is delivered. I use this technique quite often in my writing. Here's one of my favorites from my play, **The Dungeon with a View**. The play was a two-act comedy loosely based on my struggles as a young playwright in New York City. In real life, I could only afford a basement apartment. Fortunately, the apartment had a window. Unfortunately, the only view was that of people from the knees down. Borrowing from life, this was the primary set on stage.

In the second half of Act One, the main character's parents make an unannounced visit to his apartment. The mother, who is quite controlling, enters the stage admonishing the father for not putting enough quarters in the parking meter. She is convinced that this "failure to have done so" will result in serious consequences, up to and including, a long prison term. Finally, the father relinquishes and exits the stage to put more quarters in the meter.

The play has progressed to the second half of Act Two. By now, the audience has completely forgotten about the father. As the climax builds, involving the main character, his mother, his girlfriend, and his girlfriend's parents, the door opens and the long overdue father reappears. Initially, the father is unobserved by any of the characters and stands there witnessing the chaos. Then, simultaneously, his wife, son, the girlfriend, and the girlfriend's parents, all in unison, become aware of his presence; stop their arguing and stare at him. A moment of utter silence; one could hear a pin drop.

The father looks at all of them, shrugs his shoulders and says, "Okay, I'll put another quarter in the meter". And exits. The chaos resumes instantly as if the father never existed.

An aside or breaking the Fourth Wall is when a character speaks directly to an audience. Groucho Marx did this quite frequently in his plays and movies. So did Ferris Bueller in **Ferris Bueller's Day Off**. My play, **KaBoom! Or, could you please repeat that?**, was a one-act comedy I wrote shortly after I came out of the Army. **KaBoom!** was a comic book portrayed on stage with a Sgt. Rock theme. The play was unique in that the cast pre- recorded all written "sound effect" words phonetically. A tank written as *"clank, clunk, werrrrrrrr, clank, clunk, werrrrrrrr"*, was spoken, and recorded as such. The same for a hand grenade hitting the ground before exploding as *"ganork"*, or rifle shots as *"petwee, petwee, petwee"*, and so on. The recorded sounds were then played back over the sound system and timed with the action on stage. In addition, any thoughts were pre-recorded by their respective characters in the same manner.

Whenever a character would have a thought on stage, the lights would dim and a stage-hand, dressed all in black, would come on stage carrying the familiar shaped "thought bubble" seen in countless comic books. The stage-hand would cross and hold the "bubble" above the character's head and then exit upon completion of the thought which came over the sound system. At one point in the play, all six characters are having thoughts. The stage-hand is frantically bouncing back and forth from character to character as he attempts to time his activities with their thoughts. But, to no avail. Finally, exhausted, the stage-hand gives up and comes downstage, looks at the audience and says, "You want to know what I think"? And exits. **KaBoom** won the Best Comedy Award at the Bucks County Playhouse play completion in 1972.

For those not familiar with the Bucks County Playhouse, "America's Most Favorite Summer Theater", here is some interesting history. The playhouse is located in New Hope, Pennsylvania; approximately forty-five minutes north of Philadelphia. The original building was known as Hope Mills and was first constructed in 1790. The building was saved from demolition in 1930 by some of Broadway's most famous elite who purchased the run-down building and transformed it into a theater. The story supposedly went that George Kaufman, Moss Hart, Richard Rodger, Oscar Hammerstein, and others had purchased country estates in the quiet, quaint countryside to get away from the hectic life of Broadway. It wasn't long before these "giants of the theater" were bored. It was their wives who suggested they purchase the building, turn it into a playhouse, and get back to what they enjoyed doing most, the theater. So much for getting away! It should be noted that the Bucks County Playhouse is one of the finest constructed theaters in the country, rivaling anything on forty-second street. After all, who would know better than these gentlemen on how to construct a theater?

It's important that we don't take ourselves too seriously. Otherwise, life is going to be quite uncomfortable. And, not only for ourselves, but for those we will interact with during the years between cradle to grave. A sense of humor can be an alluring aphrodisiac. How many times have you heard people say that one of the qualities they look for most in a prospective partner is "a sense of humor"? If you have one, great; if you don't, develop one.

I try to make the time spent on the job as much fun as possible for myself and my colleagues. Since I specialize in "recovery", resurrecting costly and complex failed initiatives, it seems paradoxical that humor would lend itself to these situations. Yet, that's all the more reason. With the majority of these engagements, I inherit a demoralized and dysfunctional team. They lack motivation, trust, confidence, and many of the other intangibles which are essential to being successful.

Three things are necessary to bring a failed initiative back from the abyss: a deep-dive budget analysis, schedule/timeline restructuring, and a comprehensive team assessment. There are several methods to "save" the budget and timelines (which are not the focus of the book...however, you can always contract my services, and I would be glad to help).

There is only one way to "save" the team...to be blunt, some people must be let go. The number one reason for a failed initiative is failed leadership. With failed leadership come casualties. Unfortunately, there will be resources that might have otherwise been saved but have reached the point of no return. The sooner this undesirable task can be accomplished, the better for everyone involved. Once accomplished, the work of rebuilding the team can commence...with humor being a key ingredient.

I institute many unsanctioned activities to relieve stress with my teams. In the nicer weather, I'll round everyone up and say, "field trip", and then escort everyone outside into the warm sun to conduct our status meeting. Within minutes, you can see the faces of those who were feeling stressed out or feeling down due to the pressures of the job piling up, simply vanish. If the team works late, I send out for food on my dime. Most days, we sit together for lunch. No "shop talk". Lunch is a time to relax, have some laughs, and replenish one's strength. Periodically, the team goes out for an extended lunch break to a nice restaurant.

I'll send an email request to a particular team member with a slant specific to an interest they may have. I had a young team member who was a big **Mission Impossible** fan. I sent an email to him as if it was a directive from Mr. Phelps. From my office, I could see the smile forming on his face as he read my email. Although my request resulted in additional work for him, he took it on enthusiastically, as opposed to seeing it as a burden. If I could only have figured out a way to make smoke rise from his keyboard to simulate the message self-destructing, that would have been something.

As I mentioned in an earlier chapter, I *walk the floor*. If a Leader doesn't do this, they're an idiot. I was leading two large initiatives at a major hospitality corporation; one of three hospitality corporations I consulted for over my career. Combined budgets were in excess of twenty-three million dollars; the majority share of their entire budget. Not once, I repeat, not once, did the CIO ever stop into my office over a two-and-a-half year period to have a chat. In all that time, I never saw this particular CIO walk the floor. Doing so was beneath him. Jackass!

I also learn the first name of practically everyone in the building; from the maintenance crew to those who work in the cafeteria. Why? Respect! No one is beneath anyone else, no one. I have a real issue with people who have a *superior image* of themselves and believe that people have stations in life. Always take time to ask how someone is doing, and mean it. Be sincere. Be complimentary. I've been called, "the mayor" on more than one occasion and once "like I owned the place". And then there was the time I returned to the office after being absent with my sinus infection. A colleague of mine came into my office and said that with my return, it was as if "spark" ignited throughout the company. He went on to say never before had he witnessed anything like it.

I'm not sharing these stories to "pat myself on the back", I'm sharing them so that you understand the importance *you* can make in *your* organization if you *earn* people's respect.

Chapter Fourteen – "So Long, Farewell"

So long, farewell, auf wiedersehen, goodbye. Goodbye, goodbye, goodbye.

My closest friends have already retired. Called it quits. They had enough of putting up with idiots and total jackasses day-after-day. They think I'm a glutton for punishment because I haven't joined them. I see it otherwise. I'm still enjoying myself. The challenge of straightening out a huge mess, and more importantly, helping people be more successful, and leaving an indelible mark on a company's culture is still a good reason for getting up each morning.

No, I'm not a crusader out to save the world and humanity. I don't preach or lecture. I just do. George Bernard Shaw wrote: *Those who can, do. Those who can't, teach.* Woody Allen took it one step further and added: *And those who can't teach, teach gym.* Please, no letters or emails from teachers. If you feel compelled to write, then please, send your correspondence on to Woody Allen. It was his joke.

That should be everyone's goal. No, not teaching gym; but being a positive influence. Unfortunately, many people do not possess the skills, experience or, most importantly, the *nerve (I had another word in mind but I'm being nice)* to make a difference. Yes, it takes *nerve* to make a difference. For as many allies as I make on an engagement, I make as many enemies; people who feel *threatened,* others who are revealed for *just who they are,* and some who are just *plain jealous* because of my success. Like they say, "If you can't stand the heat, get out of the kitchen". I am made of asbestos. Someone has to confront the idiots. If for no other reason but that, I can't see myself retiring.

Within the first week after I took the position as a Senior Network/Systems Engineer at the private bank where I worked with the so called, "Dragon Lady", I noticed that the engineers between my group and the group that built and supported the desktop workstations were in constant battle with each other. There was a deep-rooted hatred for each other. It had become so contentious that the work-effort coming out of both groups suffered and resulted in substandard deliverables to the business community.

Starting week two, during lunch, I sat with the desktop team. Later in the afternoon, a few in my group questioned why I had lunch with the "enemy". It must have been because I was the *new kid* and didn't know any better. Quite to the contrary, I knew exactly what I was doing and continued to join the desktop team for lunch every day. One-by-one, other engineers from my group started sitting with us. Over lunch, it became apparent that the two groups weren't that different. Stories and jokes were shared; jibs were made at each other, relationships formed, and a mutual respect for each other's work and responsibilities developed. We still did battle now and then; sometimes to the point where it almost came to fisticuffs. But, at the end of the day, the best solution won out, and we'd hit a local watering hole for a few drinks and laughs to patch things up. The end result: the business community was the winner; improved deliverables, products, service, and support.

A similar situation occurred at a major pharmaceutical company. I had been engaged to help turn around two initiatives: a global deployment of a desktop image to sixty thousand users worldwide, as well as replacing two hundred MAC computers, used by their scientists, with PCs. Which do you think presented the greater challenge? Have you ever tried to take a MAC computer away from a scientist? Imagine wrestling a grizzly bear for his food. Not a pretty sight. To introduce the initiative, senior management gathered the scientists in the campus auditorium. I was actually "booed" when I walked onto the stage. Each night, I was hung in effigy outside the administrative building. I was the most hated man on campus.

As I had done before (and many times since the private bank), I joined the scientists for lunch. Some actually got up and moved to another table. This wasn't going to be easy. What finally broke the ice was when I suited up in a bio-hazard outfit and came into the lab carrying my own frog-in-a-jar (a big, rubber one). That, they appreciated! Over time, they came to realize that I wasn't going away and that I understood their concerns. I convinced them with proven, demonstrable, hard facts. After months of preparation, the day of the cut-over went without a hitch.

Resolving problems which mandate cooperation between disparate parties is one of my specialties. I was contracted by a company who had eight separate brand identities. Each brand was a recognized household name. Each brand had been allowed to do whatever they wanted from a technology perspective for years; and because of this allowance, had no commonality in accordance to development practices, hosting environments, server platforms, etc. To make things more complicated, competition amongst the brands was encouraged by the company's executive management. This "mess" didn't matter much when demand for their products was at their zenith. Quite a different story when hard times fell on American households and the money coming into the corporate coffers dried up.

Suddenly, it became paramount that a consolidation across all the Brands be done immediately. The potential savings would be in the tens-of-millions of dollars if successfully implemented. The problem was the brands had no intention of cooperating with each other. How would you handle this situation? Demanding cooperation and threatening reprisals are not options. That will get you nowhere, fast. The greatest savings were tied to the most complex initiatives. Not a good starting point. If the brands were going to learn to play nice which each other in the sandbox, the first initiative needed to be one with the least impact to their day-to-day operations and afforded each brand the greatest autonomy.

A problem which each brand had in common was keeping the maps on their websites up-to-date. Some brands used Google Maps, a few others used Virtual Earth, and one brand used a kid with a box of crayons. A "Black Box" approach was the solution. Rather than each brand continuing to code individual mapping solutions, all eight web sites would receive their maps from one location, the "Black Box". If an update and/or correction was required and applied on the "Black Box", all eight web sites would instantly be the beneficiary.

To allow individuality and sense of ownership, each brand needed to write code to connect to the "Black Box"; they would still be able to manipulate mapping controls and depict amenities of their choosing on their respective maps. The cooperation would come into play as each brand offered up how the "Black Box" should function; the pros and cons; the benefits and disadvantages to each brand's suggestions. The bottom-line? It worked. There was actually a point where one brand's application team was helping another brand's application team, who was having difficulty, write their code. Once the initial cooperation between the brands had been established, their working together became a matter-of-fact way of doing business. Now, when the teams got around to tackling the more important and critical components of consolidation, it was a unified, cohesive approach.

I'm sorry if some of you might have found this story a little long-winded while I was making my point. But, it's important that you understand how necessary it is to formulate a "strategic approach", regardless of whether you're initiating or resurrecting an initiative. Too many times, I've seen people just throw mud up against a board to see what sticks instead of planning to a destination. Do not leave anything to chance; because chances are, if you make it up as you go along, you will get lost. Men are notorious for not asking for directions (as well as a few women). Sometimes you've got to just "suck it up" and pull into a gas station.

If imitation is the sincerest form of flattery, I am indeed flattered. Quite often, when I run into someone who I've mentored in the past, they tell me how, when they are up against a troublesome situation, their initial thought is, "How would Doug handle this problem? What would Doug do or say to turn this around?" Then, they tell me they reach back in their minds to all the real-world examples they've seen me put into action, then apply the appropriate "fix". I am humbled by their kind words. Over all my engagements, inevitably, I will see people adopting my email methodology, my management style when chairing meetings, and my "straight forward" team building approach. That is my legacy.

I have achieved success and made a lot of money over the course of my career. But, money was never the objective. The objective was always to learn, grow, and have fun. Money was just an outcome. Always work smart. Smart is better than hard. And, if you work smart and hard, anything is achievable. Always be adequately compensated for your work effort. People are always looking for something for nothing. Never allow yourself to be taken advantage of. If you've acquired skills and expertise in your field of endeavor, ask for and receive every penny you are worth.

One day, a machine that made a million dollars a day broke down. The company couldn't get the machine back up and running no matter how hard they tried. After losing millions-of-dollars, they finally called in an expert to help them. The expert walked around the machine several times, pulled out a screwdriver and approached the machine. There were hundreds of exposed screws. After a few minutes, he selected one and made a slight adjustment. He then pushed the start button…the machine roared back into action.

The President of the company walked up to the expert and said, "What do we owe you?" The expert wrote up a bill and handed it to him. Looking down at the paper, the President cried out, "Ten thousand dollars. Why, that's outrageous. You were only here for ten minutes. I want this bill itemized!" The expert took back the paper and made a few changes and then handed it back to the President. The bill now read: Turning screw: one-dollar; knowing which screw to turn: nine-thousand nine-hundred ninety-nine dollars.

Most people in the workplace are good people. The key is communication and cooperation. There will always be the few bad "apples". Don't let them ruin the "work barrel" for the rest of you. It takes the collective effort of many to battle the forces of idiocy. There is strength in numbers. I remember going to grade school with a bully who was several years older than the rest of us. He was big, but not too bright; which accounted for his being left behind several years.

Each day, the bully would approach kids in the lunch line and confiscate their lunch money. While he hadn't yet approached me and my friends; we knew the day would be coming. One night, I had a conversation with my brother. I believe I suggested that he "beat the crap" out of this kid for us; a preemptive strike. My brother could have easily done that since he was the bully's same age and size and was himself, a considerable boxer. My brother said that wasn't going to resolve the problem. The problem wasn't a bully taking money; the problem was that I and my friends didn't know *"how to deal with the problem"*.

My brother went on to explain that it was obvious that the bully could easily beat up me and any one of friends, one-on-one. But, it would be impossible to take on all seven of us at the same time. Yes, one or two of us might get a bloody nose or a black-eye but, at the end of the fracas, we would be victorious, and the bully would never bother us again.

By the following week, the bully had worked his way down to where our group stood in line. He walked up to one of my friends and demanded his lunch money. Having shared my brother's conversation with "the gang", it only took a few seconds for all of us to surround him. As the designated spokesperson for the group (since it was my bright idea to do this), I informed the bully that he wasn't getting any money. Not a dime. Not from any of us; and, if he didn't like it, too bad.

I told him he'd better think twice before touching any of us; because if he did, we were all going to jump on him and "beat the crap" out of him; and not to think about getting some of us alone after school. Because we would all come after him the next chance we got and "beat the crap" out of him. He got the message loud and clear and went after less formidable prey. Do the same. Stick together at work. Watch each other's backs.

I hope I've given you some ideas and a new perspective that will help you to make your life more enjoyable. That is the ultimate success. Never forget that. Anything more is a bonus. Always help others. Be kind to one another. Don't take on some-one else's problems but do lend your support. Never stop learning.

Demonstrate confidence, not conceit. Be conscientious, but don't take yourself too seriously. Experience is the greatest teacher. Never be afraid to try new things. Be open, be receptive. Change is good. Perfection is far from being constant; quite the opposite. Only two things in this world are perfect; the sky and the ocean. Both are constantly changing. They are never the same from one moment to the next...not a single moment in time. Be like the sky, be like the ocean...change, evolve.

The Last Word: always keep a few spare light bulbs in your desk drawer. This way, when you come up against an idiot, and you will, *you* can be the one to light the way.

My best wishes for your success.

Douglas

Acknowledgements

Several people were instrumental in helping me prepare my book for publication. I am deeply thankful for the time and energies they gave to ensure that my book was ready for "prime time".

First is my wife, Patti. There is no doubt that Patti was my number one advocate...encouraging me, night after night, as I tackled the task of finding just the right words after a long day at the office. She also took on the challenge of editing and proofreading. This was by no means a small feat where my book was concerned. I write quickly so as not to lose my train-of-thought and, in doing so, have a total disregard for spelling and punctuation. Thank you, honey.

Second is Diane, who has worked with me for more than ten years as a Senior Coordinator and has lived through many of the experiences with idiots I write about. We had many a good laugh when a "light bulb" would go off at a meeting or some other office interaction that signified we just had an "idiot encounter". Diane also leant her expertise editing, proofreading, and formatting. Thank you, Diane.

Third are two very dear friends, Lisa and Laurie, who Diane and I have had the pleasure to work with several times. It should be noted that both Lisa and Laurie have lifelong memberships at Club Doug. Lisa and Laurie also helped to edit, proofread, and critique. The book was improved with their insights and constructive suggestions. I will always be grateful. Thank you, Lisa and Laurie.

Now, on to my "best friends". While they didn't edit, proofread, or critique, they were instrumental in the writing of this book. After all, they are an integral part of who I am. Three friendships span fifty-five years; two, fifty years; and one, more than fifteen years. Frank, Dieter, Rainer, Roy, Jim, and Nick know me better than anyone else on the planet...and, amazingly, after all these years, we still like each other. To this day, we do our best to see each other as often as we can. It should be known, that our wives, after hearing our *many stories time and time again*, took it upon themselves to "numbering" them. Now when telling a story, we simply hold up a few fingers instead of saying a single word...an enormous time (and marriage) saver. I love you, guys!

The Ten Business Commandments

Thou shalt not worship false idols and condone idiots in the workplace.

Thou shalt not speak the name of the author of this book in vain.

Thou shall keep weekends for thyself and take vacations.

Thou shall only honor thy manager and other team members who are not total jackasses.

Thou shalt not kill time being lazy and non-productive.

Thou shall act as an adult, always respectful of others.

Thou shalt never steal and take credit for someone else's work.

Thou shalt not lay blame for his/her mistakes onto others.

Thou shalt not covet a co-worker's position through subversive means.

Thou shall earn the respect of others, each day, and every day.

.

Chapter Title Credits

I thought using song titles as chapter titles might be an interesting alternative to how chapters are typically titled. For those of you who may be curious, I've listed the song titles, along with their respective songwriters. Can you remember who performed these songs? While some are obvious, others may pose a challenge.
Good luck!

Chapter One – *Don't Worry, Be Happy*
Words & music by Bob Marley

Chapter Two – *It Was a Very Good Year*
Words & music by Ervin Drake

Chapter Three – *Back Stabbers*
Words & music by Leon Huff, Gene McFadden & John Whitehead

Chapter Four – *Who Will Buy*
Words & music by Lionel Bart

Chapter Five – *Getting To Know You*
Words by Oscar Hammerstein; Music by Richard Rodgers

Chapter Six – *Just the Way You Are*
Words & music by Billy Joel

Chapter Seven – *You've Got to Be Taught*
Words by Oscar Hammerstein; Music by Richard Rodgers

Chapter Eight – *The Meeting Song*
Words & music by Linda Chobotuck

Chapter Title Credits cont....

Chapter Nine – *Return To Sender*
Words & music by Otis Blackwell and Winfield Scott

Chapter Ten – *Every Breath You Take*
Words & music by Sting

Chapter Eleven – *Just Once in a Lifetime*
Words & music by Anthony Newley and Leslie Bricusse

Chapter Twelve – *The Long and Winding Road*
Words & music by John Lennon and Paul McCartney

Chapter Thirteen – *Make 'em Laugh*
Words by Arthur Freed; Music by Nacio Herb Brown

Chapter Fourteen – *So Long, Farewell*
Words by Oscar Hammerstein; Music by Richard Rodgers

Made in United States
Troutdale, OR
01/15/2024

16938006R00116